How to Sell

Books that make you better

Books that make you better – that make you *be* better, *do* better, *feel* better. Whether you want to upgrade your personal skills or change your job, whether you want to improve your managerial style, become a more powerful communicator, or be stimulated and inspired as you work.

Prentice Hall Business is leading the field with a new breed of skills, careers and development books. Books that are a cut above the mainstream – in topic, content and delivery – with an edge and verve that will make you better, with less effort.

Books that are as sharp and smart as you are.

Prentice Hall Business.
We work harder – so you don't have to.

For more details on products, and to contact us, visit
www.pearsoned.co.uk

How to Sell

Sell anything to anyone

Jo Owen

Prentice Hall
Business
is an imprint of

Harlow, England • London • New York • Boston • San Francisco • Toronto
Sydney • Tokyo • Singapore • Hong Kong • Seoul • Taipei • New Delhi
Cape Town • Madrid • Mexico City • Amsterdam • Munich • Paris • Milan

PEARSON EDUCATION LIMITED

Edinburgh Gate
Harlow CM20 2JE
Tel: +44 (0)1279 623623
Fax: +44 (0)1279 431059
Website: www.pearsoned.co.uk

First published in Great Britain in 2010

© Jo Owen 2010

The right of Jo Owen to be identified as author of this work has been asserted
by him in accordance with the Copyright, Designs and Patents Act 1988.

Pearson Education is not responsible for the content of third party internet sites.

ISBN: 978-0-273-73127-6

British Library Cataloguing-in-Publication Data
A catalogue record for this book is available from the British Library

Library of Congress Cataloging-in-Publication Data
Owen, Jo.
  How to sell : sell anything to anyone / Jo Owen.
    p. cm.
  Includes index.
  ISBN 978-0-273-73127-6 (pbk.)
  1. Selling. I. Title
  HF5438.25.O94 2010
  658.85--dc22
                    2010018253

Printed in Great Britain by Ashford Colour Press Ltd
ARP Impression 98

Cartoons by Roger Beale
Typeset in 10pt Plantin by 30

Contents

About the author

Jo Owen started his sales career by selling his own blood in Afghanistan. He then became the best nappy salesperson in Birmingham. He has successfully sold in Japan without speaking any Japanese. In 30 years he has sold professional services across Asia, the Middle East, Europe and North America in most major industries. He has even started and sold a bank.

He is the author of several management best sellers, including *How to Lead* and *How to Manage*. In his teaching and writing he has already helped over 100,000 managers and salespeople become more effective. He has featured on CNN and the BBC, in *The Wall Street Journal*, *Financial Times* and many magazines and newspapers, and has presented two television series on leadership.

Jo Owen practises what he preaches. Aside from his sales practice, he is the co-founder of four national charities, including Teach First, which is now one of the top ten graduate recruiters in the UK. He was a partner at Accenture, built a business in Japan, was sued for $12 billion and is now the managing partner of the Leadership Partnership.

In his spare time he has spent seven years with traditional societies finding out what modern business can learn from them; the results are published in *Tribal Business School*. He is in demand as a speaker and can be contacted at Speakers for Business.

Introduction

Many years ago I went into a grocery store on my first formal sales call. The store manager took one look at me and threw me out of the store before I could even open my mouth. Welcome to the world of selling.

This was the normal apprenticeship that Procter & Gamble gave its bright-eyed graduates. It was the best apprenticeship anyone could have. It not only built resilience, it taught the most important skill that anyone can learn: how to sell.

Selling is as easy as kicking a football; anyone can do it, but doing it well takes hard work and practice. And the good news is that anyone *can* learn to sell well if they want to. You do not have to be born to sell, with charisma and a patter from the day you come into this world.

Most of us learn selling through the apprenticeship model. We observe other salespeople in action, and learn from their successes and failures. If we are lucky, we have good role models and learn fast. If we are unlucky, the random walk of experience leads into career dead ends. That is where *How to Sell* will help. It lets you gain an insight into the experience of the very best salespeople around the world. There is little theory in *How to Sell*: this is a book based on hard-won experience, both good and bad. It lets you remove some of the randomness from the random walk of personal experience; it gives you structure so you can accelerate your learning from your sales experience.

Unlike most sales books, *How to Sell* does not assume that all selling is the same. Selling to a government minister or to a CEO is different from selling to consumers in a shop. But there are some common principles behind all sales situations. *How to Sell* distils the essence of selling and then shows how the principles of selling can be applied in different situations: selling to consumers, to key accounts, in relationship management and in bid situations.

Over the last 30 years I have helped over 100,000 managers and salespeople improve their performance. Just as important, I have been able to learn from them as well. *How to Sell* is the essence of all their knowledge, wisdom and experience.

Opposite is a short list of a few of the organisations I have been privileged to work with. I hope they gained as much from the relationship as I did. My thanks to them all.

Accenture	Mitsubishi Chemical
Airbus	Monsanto
American Express	National Air Traffic Services
ANZ Bank	Norwegian Dairy Association
Armstrong World Industries	Philips
Barclays Bank	RHM
BASF	Procter & Gamble
BT	Royal & Sun Alliance
Capgemini	SABIC
Cisco Systems	San Miguel
Citibank	SDP
Cognitas	Skype
EDS	SWIFT
Hallmark Cards	Symantec
HCA	Teach First
ITOCHU	Teaching Leaders
Lloyds TSB Bank	UBS
MAC Group	Unilever
Merrill Lynch	Union Carbide
MetLife	ZFS

Part 1

The principles of selling

To understand how to sell, we must first understand how people buy. Fortunately, this is easy to do. We have all bought things. Sometimes we have enjoyed the experience, sometimes not. Take a moment to think about some of these experiences for yourself. Here is my experience of buying a new computer recently.

I entered the store, which had a dazzling array of computers and offers. It was overwhelming. I had gone in with some clear ideas about what I wanted to buy and how much I wanted to spend, but suddenly I felt confused. After about five minutes of wandering around, my eyes had glazed over and I was staring blankly into the middle distance: my mind was numbed by too much choice.

Suddenly there was a voice in my ear. 'Interested in the Sony?' asked the voice. I quickly took my hand off the Sony and mumbled something incoherent. The voice was off to the races, extolling the virtues of the Sony. It certainly sounded like an amazing computer.

After about five minutes I finally got a word in edgeways. 'Actually, I was hoping for something a bit cheaper' I said. Immediately the voice switched to an own-label brand, which was much cheaper and sounded just as good as the Sony.

By now I had made my mind up. There was no way I was going to buy anything at this store. More to the point, there was no way I would buy anything from the salesperson behind the voice. I made my excuses and scuttled out of the store.

As I left, I wondered what had gone wrong. The store had a good selection and good prices. The salesperson had clearly been sales trained. He knew his products, could sell their benefits, could counter any objections I had and he certainly knew a few ways of trying to close. And he was persistent.

Despite all his technique, I realised I just did not trust the salesperson. So what had gone wrong?

- He did not listen: he talked at me and down to me.
- He gave me no space.
- He was all hype, while I wanted the facts.
- He seemed more interested in selling than in helping me.
- He said 'Trust me': I never trust anyone who says 'Trust me'.

Logically, the store probably had the right deal for me, if I had been prepared to negotiate. But the risk of getting the wrong deal on the wrong product was too great. Too much risk and too little trust guarantee a 'no sale'.

A few days later I plucked up courage to go to another store. It was déjà vu. Another dazzling and confusing display of computers and offers. As my eyes glazed over and my heart sank, another voice appeared at my shoulder. The voice introduced himself as the store's computer whizz and asked me what I was wanting from my computer. I explained and the whizz listened. He then asked me more questions, which I had not even thought of. Finally, he asked about my budget, which I reckoned at £750 all in: computer, peripherals, software, warranties.

The whizz thought for a couple of moments and then picked out two computers which he thought might be of interest. First he recommended a package that came to about £575. Well below my budget: I was impressed. Here was someone I could trust. I asked about the alternative. The whizz hesitated. 'It's a bit above your budget. I could do it at £25 a month for 36 months. But this is why it might work for you ...' He then showed how it fitted my expressed needs perfectly. Finally, he shuffled slightly awkwardly and said: 'Look, I know it's a bit beyond your budget. But if you go for the more expensive option, I might be able to extend the warranty to three years for you.'

> he showed how it fitted my expressed needs perfectly

It was a simple decision. I opted for the more expensive package. It met my needs and I trusted the whizz with his clear advice. Logically, I knew I did not need the extended warranty, but I really liked it, because free is good.

So what had the computer whizz done right? He was not even a salesperson: he was a computer whizz. But he had sold me a more expensive package than I had been budgeting for. He may not have been a trained salesperson, but he showed how anyone can sell if they have the right attitude and approach. As I hauled my computer across the car park, I thought about why I had bought from him:

1 He listened to and understood my needs.
2 He appeared to help me, rather than sell to me.
3 He focused on me, not on his sales commission.
4 He seemed to be an expert, but he did not talk down to me.
5 He gave me space to talk and think.
6 He gave me a restricted, simple choice: even I can choose between two options.
7 He talked about the benefits to me of each computer, not just their boring technical features.

8   He built trust by offering me the lower price choice first: that showed he respected my needs and budget.

9   He even closed me with the offer of the extended warranty, which gave me a story to tell to my family to prove that I had got a good bargain: I would not look like a fool for trading up.

10 He was positive and enthusiastic throughout.

So if you want to succeed, you need more than just technique. Knowing ten ways to close, to price-qualify a prospect and how to overcome objections are all good techniques to have. But the more we appear to be selling, the less we are trusted. The computer whizz did not think of himself as a salesperson: he thought of himself as an expert. Good salespeople often appear to be more of a selfless expert than a commission-hungry salesperson.

As I drove the computer home, I realised that the computer whizz was doing naturally what I had been trying to learn for years: how to sell well. He may not have had all the techniques, but he had a great approach. I now keep the whizz in my mind when talking to clients and prospects, and follow his approach:

1   Listen.

2   Help more than sell.

3   Focus on the client's needs, not on my needs.

4   Be expert, but don't talk down.

5   Give the client time and space.

6   Make it simple for the client: avoid confusion through too much choice.

7   Focus on benefits to the client, not features of the product.

8   Build trust, but never say 'Trust me'.

9   Give the client a story to tell their peers that shows that they bought smart and got a good deal.

10 Be positive and enthusiastic throughout.

Of course, there are still many creative ways to mess up any sales situation: to sell is to discover the full range of bizarre human nature. And that is what makes it both fun and frustrating at the same time. But by following the ten steps of the computer whizz it is hard to go too far wrong.

Of course, some technique is also required. And that is what this book is all about: it explores the techniques and approaches you can use in the different sorts of sales situations you are likely to encounter: bids, key account management, relationship management and retail selling.

At the heart of sales technique itself is the sale, which is no more than a persuasive conversation. This is not like old-fashioned selling: that is often seen as an adversarial contest where you bludgeon the buyer into submission by qualifying the buyer, overcoming objections and closing the sale. Nor is it a social conversation, which is a random walk. The persuasive conversation has a clear structure which you manage and allows you to help the buyer buy from you. At the end of the persuasive conversation, you will not just have made a sale: you will have made a willing customer who wants to come back to you time and again.

Chapter 1

Preparing to succeed

Selling is more exciting than preparing. Just like hunting, most of us prefer the thrill of the chase to the tedium of preparation. But hunting rarely succeeds without adequate preparation. Even our Neolithic ancestors understood this: make sure you are hunting the right animals the right way at the right time with the right team and right weapons. Some salespeople are so keen on the hunting that they under-prepare. Other salespeople, who are scared of the hunt, spend their whole time preparing: it is useful avoidance activity. The quality, not quantity of preparation is what counts, and the bigger the sale, the better you must prepare.

Generals claim that most battles are won and lost before the first shot is fired, and the same is true of sales conversations. If you are talking to the right person at the right time about the right topic in the right way, you have to work hard to fail. Equally, if you talk with the wrong person at the wrong time about the wrong subject in the wrong way, then no matter how much genius you have in sales techniques, you are likely to come away empty-handed. Preparation is not everything, but without it you are nothing.

The six key questions of a successful sale

Preparation is about answering the basic questions which any journalist has to answer when writing a story: who, what, where, when, how and why. Elliott Carver, the villain in the James Bond film *Tomorrow Never Dies*, told of how he had started out as a journalist on a rag of a newspaper in Hong Kong and had been taught to answer those basic questions. 'But,' he said, 'by far the most interesting question is "why?"' Answering the 'why' question took him to the cusp of world domination. You may not achieve world domination by asking who, what, where, when, how and why, but you will certainly improve your prospects of selling.

So if we follow the Elliott Carver principle, sales preparation requires answering the following questions:

- What?
- How?
- When?
- Who?
- Where?
- Why?

The questions may be easy, but the answers are not easy. Preparing well means going beyond the superficial answers to each question, as we shall discover below.

What?

This is obvious, isn't it? Buyers are buying a television, or a car, or a consulting project. Surely we know what people are buying, don't we?

You have to look far beyond the logical sell of the product. People do not just buy a car: they are expressing their identity. Logically, they do not need a car that goes faster than the speed limit, or has off-road capabilities when they live in the city. But fast cars and off-road cars are hugely popular: buying is not just about logic, and nor is selling. In similar fashion, people did not just buy a set of very expensive encyclopaedias. They were buying knowledge, education, hope and prospects for their children. To succeed, you have to reach beyond the logical sale to the emotional sale. This is as true of big corporate selling as it is of retailing selling, although with a twist.

The two keys to answering the 'what' question are:

- features, benefits, hopes and dreams;
- the art of the story.

Features, benefits, hopes and dreams

I was selling groceries in some gritty, blue-collar towns in Northern England. Grocery selling is a pretty rational business, or so I thought. Each detergent met a different need: Daz washes whiter; Dreft is good for wool and delicate fabrics; Ariel is tough on stains. But then I started noticing the Fairy Liquid bottles. About half the blue-collar homes I passed had a bottle of Fairy Liquid displayed prominently in the kitchen window, above the kitchen sink. At first I dismissed this as a bizarre northern habit, but then I moved south and saw the same thing going on. Eventually, I worked it out. Fairy Liquid is the most up-market washing liquid you can buy. It always sells at a few pennies premium to its nearest rivals, and always portrays itself as top quality. So putting the Fairy Liquid in your kitchen window is a very cheap way of saying that you have high standards, and that you are house-proud. Anyone who buys a cheap dishwashing liquid keeps it out of sight. Even basic items have an emotional sale attached to them.

When selling, we are typically selling at three levels at the same time. We are selling:

- features;
- benefits;
- hopes and dreams.

To understand the difference, think of buying or selling a car. A car is packed full of features, such as engine size, fuel consumption, safety features, conveniences such as GPS and air conditioning. These are all features of the car, and they stay the same whoever we are selling to. Some people may get wildly excited when told about torque, engine capacity and the number of carburettors. For most of us, that is dull stuff. In practice we are not just buying a set of features which we carefully evaluate with a cost/benefit analysis. We are buying an identity.

As salespeople, we know that cars are about identity: they represent ourselves and our hopes and our dreams. At one time I had to redesign the pay and benefits of the sales force. This is potentially dangerous territory: you are messing with people's incomes and livelihoods. Each proposal was inevitably met with a chorus of disapproval from the team members who thought they might lose, while the potential winners all kept quiet. After a while, I figured out how I could make the change stick. Of course, the new pay and bonus structure had to be sensible; it had to be explained and training had to be offered so that everyone could win in the new world. But the killer was the car. I offered a very modest upgrade to every car when it was due for renewal, if the team went along with the pay changes. Suddenly, sweetness and light broke out. I had given the team what they really wanted.

> cars are about identity: they represent our hopes and our dreams

We all want to succeed and want to be seen to succeed. Within the company, there are plenty of ways of doing this: competitions, prizes, award ceremonies and the like. Outside the company, it is much harder to show how successful you are. Salary, like death and sex, is not discussed in polite company. But cars can be discussed, and they are a very visible symbol of success or otherwise. Offering all my sales team a car upgrade was like offering them a social upgrade with all their friends and family. The features of the car, like torque and acceleration, were irrelevant. We were tapping into the hopes and dreams of everyone in the team, at very low cost.

Think about selling cars, and how they are marketed in the media. Around half the big off-road cars sold in the UK are sold within the M25, the motorway that encircles London. And most of these large off-road cars never venture beyond the city. And yet there is not much call for driving off the road in the middle of the city. So why are off-road vehicles so popular? If you map out the features, benefits and hopes and dreams of an off-road car, it soon becomes clear what people are really buying.

Features	Benefits	Hopes and dreams
Four-wheel drive	Gets through mud	Look adventurous
Air conditioning	Comfortable	Be sophisticated
Six-litre engine	Powerful	'Mine is bigger than yours …'
High driving position	Safe for me and the kids	Look down on everyone else

Clearly, you will find a subtler way of hinting at the hopes and dreams column in the table. Talking about who else has bought the car (celebrity explorers to metropolitan media celebrities) and referring to the expeditions on which the cars have been used will quietly reinforce the self-image the buyer is looking for.

From dishwashing liquid to off-road cars, we can see how people buy more than features. They buy hopes and dreams. These hopes and dreams are not private fantasies: they are normally dreams about how friends, neighbours and colleagues see the buyer. It is about constructing a story in which the buyer is the hero, or at least is never the fool. If you can craft the right story, you can win the sale.

The art of the story

I had an aunt who owned a sweet shop. When you are eight years old, life does not get better than that. Auntie Baba was my very favourite aunt in the whole, whole world.

Auntie Baba decided to introduce me to the world of behavioural economics, which was surprising because at that time the term did not even exist. If she had worked in Chicago as an economist, instead of Newark selling sweets, she would have won a Nobel Prize for her work. Selling sweets to children gives you a keen understanding of human nature that economists miss completely.

One of her lessons involved the idea of choice and regret. When I visited she would normally offer me a choice between two sorts of sweet, which she would have selected for me. Her selection was pretty good: she had plenty of other eight-year-olds to observe. It was usually a pretty easy choice and I would happily focus on becoming hyperactive and obese with whatever tooth rot I had selected.

One day, she changed the rules. I could have any sweet from the entire shop. Bliss! My eyes grew as wide as saucers as I contemplated my choice. I must have taken ages checking out all the jars and packages and trying to work out which would be the best. I could sense that even the ever-patient Auntie Baba was getting impatient. So I made a decision: Milky Bars. And I immediately regretted the decision. I was convinced that I must have missed the best choice. There were hundreds of options out there: should I have picked the gobstoppers, or the allsorts, or the humbugs or the sherbet? Heaven descended into hell as I thought about all the missed opportunities out there. My Milky Bars suddenly had a sour taste as I thought about what I might have had.

Behavioural economists would recognise this problem immediately (now that they know they exist). It is the problem of choice and regret. The more choice we have, the more likely we are to regret the choice. With a limited choice, we can be fairly sure we made the right choice. With unlimited choice, we can be fairly sure we missed the best choice somewhere.

So what has this got to do with selling? Everything.

The first and obvious conclusion is: don't give people too much choice. The more choice they have, the more confused they become and the more likely they are to make no choice at all. The 'alternate close' is a great way of closing a sale and gaining agreement: it is normally a choice between two options, not between 200 options. Closed options works better than open options.

The second conclusion is that buyers need reassurance: they need to know they are making a good choice. Buying is stressful, and the greater the choice, the greater the stress. We all fear going home after a big purchase and finding that our neighbour or colleague got a better deal or a better price. The financial cost is irrelevant: the social cost is mortifying: we have just been exposed as a poor buyer.

> buying is stressful, and the greater the choice, the greater the stress

So we are not just selling a product or a service. We are selling a story. At the heart of the story is a very simple message: 'You are a smart buyer who has made a smart choice. You will not be embarrassed by your decision.' The key is that you are *not* selling a story about yourself or your product. You are creating a story that the buyer can tell to friends and colleagues.

The power of the story works in both retail and business sales.

In business selling, the same problem arises. There is so much ambiguity about buying things like professional services it becomes very hard to make a fully rational decision. This was clear when I was a partner at Accenture (when it was still called Andersen Consulting). It struck me that the firm could not claim to be the cheapest, or the quickest, or the most innovative. And yet clients were knocking at our doors demanding our services: it was the easiest selling anyone could dream of doing. So what were the very sophisticated customers of Accenture buying, if not price, speed or innovation? They were buying safety. If you hire Accenture, you will not be regarded as a fool: it is not a career-limiting move. If you hire a cheaper, quicker, better and more innovative boutique you might be a hero. But you put your career on the line: if the boutique messes up, wave goodbye to your bonus, promotion and job.

For Accenture clients, the story they construct is simple: 'I am a prudent and safe custodian of the firm's IT.' Accenture might negotiate things like price, scope and timing, but what it is selling is different from what it is negotiating.

The same principle applies in most situations. Selling office copiers at one level is a rational discussion about speed, features, price, service and reliability. But most buyers of copiers are not experts at buying copiers: they have other things to worry about in their lives. So buying a copier is a fear-based purchase. If I buy a copier which is useless, everyone in the office is going to give me grief every day for the next year. Every secretary will hate me; every mangled or late copy will be my fault. Ouch.

Selling copiers successfully is an art form and works at several levels:

- **Features**. These include the speed, reliability etc. of the copier. The features of the copier remain the same, whoever you talk to.

- **Benefits**. These are how the copier will make life better, more efficient, cheaper and more professional looking for your staff and organisation. The benefits of the copier depend on what the client is looking for: benefits start by understanding the customer, not the product.

- **Hopes and dreams**. You will look good in front of your staff and management if you buy this copier. This is where the story comes in: you will look good because it is an improvement on what you have now; because you drove a great bargain; because it will not be a lemon and embarrass you.

> the buyer needs reassurance that they have done well

You cannot succeed by defeating clients. Instead, let clients think that they have won. Help them celebrate their success with their friends and colleagues by giving them the story of their success. No sale is a purely rational sale; it has to work as an emotional success as well. The buyer needs reassurance that they have done well: give them what they want.

So what do you really sell?

Typically, the weaker salespeople sell features. These are the people who have fallen in love with their product and can talk about nothing else. This is a huge trap that many salespeople fall into. It is easy to talk about features: you know them and they do not change. But pitching and pushing features is a turn-off to most buyers. They want to talk about their needs, not listen to your pitch.

Effective salespeople learn to move from talking about features to discussing benefits. Features of the product remain the same, whoever you talk to. But the benefits change depending on each buyer: that means that a benefits discussion is as much about listening to the customer as talking to the customer.

Great salespeople go beyond benefits to selling hopes and dreams. To achieve this, you must listen both to what the customer says, and to what the customer leaves unsaid. Customers rarely talk about their hopes, fears and dreams openly. But when you understand this, you are well on the way to success.

How?

If you ask people how they buy a product or service, they will lie to you. This is not because they are unpleasant or want to deceive you. Customers will lie to you out of politeness. They will tell you what you want to hear, not what you need to hear. They will lie because they themselves do not understand how they are buying. If you understand how they arrive at their decision, you are one step ahead of the buyer. This is your secret weapon.

Even in the retail world, people do not understand how they buy. For instance, we worked with one firm to understand how people buy mobile phones. If we could understand this, we could sell more. The firm had lots of consumer research that told them that consumers are rational. The research said the consumers work out what combination of texts, internet, voice, email and other applications they use. Then they find the phone at the lowest cost with the best features for their usage. All highly rational and highly untrue.

We suspected that the answers were not right: it certainly did not gel with the way that customers seemed to behave in store. So we changed our approach. We talked to people as they left the store. We stopped asking for their attitudes. Attitudinal questions are things like:

● Why did you buy?

● Why did you not buy?

If you ask for attitudes, people give you the answers they think they are meant to give: they think they are meant to buy rationally, so that is what they will tell you.

Instead, we started asking them about their behaviour. Behaviour questions include:

● How many stores have you visited?

● How much did you spend?

● Which (named) magazines or websites did you look at before coming out?

● Which product was the nearest competitor? Why did you not choose it?

● What are you going to tell your friends/family about the purchase when you get back home?

The answers were a revelation. We found that:

● The more research customers did, the more confused they became by all the choice.

● Customers found great difficulty in comparing products: they could not even reliably recall the details or even the price of what they had just bought.

- They all constructed a story in their heads about how they had got a great deal and that is what they would tell their friends and family: they wanted bragging rights.

- They all wanted a phone that would look good compared to their friends or colleagues.

- Most of the time, customers just wanted a friendly expert to make the decision easy for them.

We had been selling on price and features. We changed tack. The store still had the big red posters up shouting about sales and bargains: that reassured the customers around price. But we moved from selling to advising: we became the friendly experts who listened more than they talked. We never looked back.

When people are asked how they buy, they come up with rational answers, because that is what they are meant to do. To sell well, you need a deeper understanding of how people buy. Most purchases are not just rational: they are emotional and political.

most purchases
are not just rational:
they are emotional
and political

For retail customers, there is always an emotional element to a purchase: 'Will this purchase make me look good, does it fit my self-image, will I look smart for having driven a good bargain?' For business customers, there is also the emotional element of wanting to look good in front of peers; but there is also a deeply political element in making sure that all the power barons and competing constituencies are kept happy.

In theory, it should be clearer how large organisations buy. For instance, the public sector prides itself on the transparency of its tendering process. That means it is a bureaucratic nightmare, with officials asking endless, and often arcane and irrelevant questions. On a good day, bureaucrats are led by the twin stars of fairness and efficiency. Meanwhile, back on planet earth, they are often led by the need to protect their backs and minimise their risk. The rational process they slavishly follow can be blown away by the political needs of their masters. The private sector can be as arcane, but in different ways. The different sorts of buying process are covered in depth in Part 2 of this book, which looks at key account management, relationship management and bids and tenders.

When?

There are three principles behind the 'when' question:

- be early;
- work the sales cycle;
- seize the right moment.

Be early

Daniel was one of the brightest people I ever met. He also worked incredibly hard. He had a view that if he did not miss at least one flight in ten, then he was wasting his time. He cut everything down to the last minute. It was very stressful working with him: he worked too hard, smoked too much and died too young.

In contrast, Mark is one of the idler salespeople I have worked with. At least he appears that way. If there is a big sales meeting he has to go to, he aims to arrive an hour in advance. When he drives there, he is not worrying about traffic jams and getting there on time. He is rehearsing the meeting and preparing himself. Even if there are traffic problems, he will still get there on time and will not be stressed out on arrival. And by arriving early, he gets the chance to check the place out, read the company literature and pick up any hints that might help in his call. He does not do many meetings, but each one tends to be a knock-out success. He sells well and lives well: no chance of an early death for him.

Work the sales cycle

There is a sales cycle for more or less everything. Some products are seasonal: to this day Flash and other household cleaners get promoted heavily around the spring-cleaning season, even though the spring-cleaning ritual has largely disappeared. When selling leadership programmes, remember that most organisations go through a three-year cycle. Every three years a new executive in HR is appointed to develop the leadership programme, so they make their mark by changing suppliers and design. Within three years, the organisation gets bored with the arrangement, the executive moves on and they start again. You have to sell at the transition point: selling against an established programme that has two years to run is a waste of time.

Seize the right moment

There are moments when people are ready to buy, and moments when they are not. Lenny is a particularly manic CEO. He comes into work like a demented toy soldier on a Monday morning. He has wound himself up over the weekend and is spewing out orders non-stop in a whirl of activity on Monday. Over the week, he slowly unwinds. By Friday afternoon, he has chilled out. Friday afternoon is when all the other executives make an early departure and Lenny is left to his devices in his office. I acquired the habit of staying late on Fridays and chilling out with him. No one in the organisation could understand how I always seemed to be able to sell anything to him, while they all struggled to survive. Timing, as any good waiter knows, is everything.

Who?

This question is less obvious than it may seem. I have seen estate agents busily selling to the husband, while the wife quietly makes the real decision. I have seen brilliant sales efforts convince a senior manager to buy a multi-million-pound contract, only to discover that the real decision lay elsewhere in the organisation. Even official tender documents can be wildly misleading: public sector procurement is a minefield of misinformation. The tender document will lay out in tedious detail the entire procurement process; how questions can be asked, how many points each section of the bid will be allocated, timings and how the decision will be arrived at. Junior civil servants then follow the irrelevant procedure. Meanwhile a quiet word with the Secretary of State, who officially has nothing to do with the process, works a mysterious magic: miraculously the result is what you wanted it to be.

assume nothing, because assumptions are deadly

This raises the obvious question: how do you know who the buyer is? The easy answer is that you don't know. Assume nothing, because assumptions are deadly. If you are selling in a retail store, there is little you can do to prepare: you have to observe, ask, listen and make no assumptions before you start any sales conversation.

In a complex business-to-business sales environment, things are not so simple. There will not be one buyer. There will be many buyers who all have a different role to play. You may find up to six different roles being played. In a healthy relationship, you know all of them and what their needs are:

- **Economic buyer**. This is the person we often think of as the decision maker. They may well orchestrate the decision-making process, but they will rarely make a decision alone: that could be a career-limiting move. They will want the support of their organisation, and you can help them achieve that support.

- **Authoriser**. This is normally the most senior person involved in the process: their involvement may be small (in time) but critical (in impact). Find out who this is and what their agenda is: often their intentions are garbled as messages go down through the organisation. Show that you have the authoriser on your side, and the rest of the organisation will mysteriously fall in line behind you: people do not fight battles with their boss or the boss of their boss.

- **Technical buyers**. These are the people who cannot say yes, but they can say no. They often exist in finance, health and safety, legal and other staff functions. Seek them out early, get on their side and make your pitch consistent with their arcane needs.

- **Influencers**. These shadowy figures may appear insubstantial, but ignore them at your peril. They might be planning managers, mentors or apparently harmless people, but their views may be valued by the other buyers if they have experience and are seen to be impartial. Bring them on board early and have them whispering in your favour: they may even be able to coach you through the politics of the organisation.

- **Gatekeepers**. Never underrate a secretary. They have diary power: if they are on your side, impossible schedules suddenly get relaxed for you. If they are against you, the diary seems perpetually closed.

- **Users**. These are the people who will actually use your product, even if they do not have the power to buy it. Understand their real needs and you will able to cast the decision-making criteria in a way that is favourable to you: you will look like you are speaking sense and understanding the real needs of the organisation rather than responding to a bland tender document.

Working a buying network takes serious effort, and is covered in detail in Chapter 6 on relationship management. It is often a team effort. Your job is not to be a hero: it is to sell. Do not try to do it all yourself; get whatever support is required to make the sale succeed.

Where?

Most of the time there is a very obvious answer to this question: you sell wherever the customer is and wherever the customer wants to meet. In practice, that means that unless you work in a retail store or call centre you are likely to be nomadic. Even grand consulting partners or senior bankers find themselves on planes, trains and taxis meeting clients at their offices. Partners are the highly paid gypsies of the corporate world: going wherever they can to earn a penny or two.

> a little power makes little people into little tyrants

But the obvious answer is not the whole answer. 'Where' is about territory, power and emotion. If I am a customer and we meet on my territory, then I feel in control. That is good for me, and it puts me in the power position. I will act as judge and jury, as many buyers like to do: a little power makes little people into little tyrants.

Too many buyers like playing their power games. If I meet on your territory, for instance if I go into your shop, I will be on guard. I will be guarding against a sales ambush: being rushed into buying something I may regret later.

Occasionally, it makes sense to find a neutral venue. No one controls the territory here, and for once both buyer and seller can meet on equal terms. They can get to know each other and understand each other better. This is partly why corporate entertaining is so popular: it takes people out of the normal business context and creates a more collaborative environment. The ideal event is one where you get plenty of time to get drunk and talk with each other.

Lunch is good, dinner is better and a whole weekend is the jackpot. I was once invited to go shooting with some industry big shots. As a rule, guns scare me and gun owners scare me even more. I thought that if I went shooting, at least all the grouse would be perfectly safe: I had no chance of hitting any, even if I had wanted to. So I went. By the end of the weekend, all the big shots had convinced themselves that the world would be a far better place if only it was run by decent people like themselves. They had achieved perfect alignment. More importantly, they were all ready to do business with each other, because they now trusted each other. Doors that had been firmly shut to me suddenly started opening up.

There are some basic rules about entertaining:

- **Fit the situation**. You can be too lavish (looks like bribery) and too mean. Pitch it right for each client.
- **Make it personal**. Find an event that is of real interest to the client: football for someone who hates football is not smart.
- **Be different**. Find a venue or event that is unusual. Intrigue the client and give them bragging rights when they get back to the office. Lunch at a restaurant is instantly forgettable, unless the menu includes fried ants and scorpion. The scorpion was rubbery, the ants were crispy. Neither was forgettable.

- **Focus on the person, not on the business**. You gain most by building emotional engagement with the client, not by trying to do deals at the opera. If the client wants to talk business, fine. Otherwise, build rapport: there is plenty of time later to talk business.

Why?

'Why' is more than just a question. It is a state of mind. It is about always challenging assumptions, reviewing why we succeeded or failed. 'Why' encompasses all the other questions about who, what, when and how, but forces us to step back and challenge ourselves. The typical questions to ask include:

- Why does the buyer want to buy? Why now? Why at all?
- Why would they want to buy from me – and why not?
- Why would they not buy from the competition – why might they?
- Why did they just say that to me?

Asking 'why' repeatedly helps in two ways:

- It increases your success rate on individual sales.
- It is a way of constantly learning and developing your mastery of sales practice.

A real-life example will show how the 'why' question makes the difference between success and failure.

We were starting a new education programme. We had nearly all the approvals. There was only one more person we needed to convince: the education minister. It was a big sale. If we got it, we could create hundreds of jobs. If we did not get it, the enterprise would go under. And we could not sell to anyone else: there was only one buyer and our future depended on it. Not much pressure then …

We did all the homework. We lined up all his advisers and staff to support us, and we worked the networks. We got to the big meeting. The minister walked in. 'Sorry, it's all off' he said, and walked out again without further discussion. Time for the 'why' question. We turned to his advisers, who were still in the room and asked. They told us that, on reflection, they realised that the programme was too risky: if it failed it would cost money and embarrass the minister. The advisers then left us to mull over our disaster.

The obvious response would be to rework our proposal to make sure that it was a risk-free, 100-per-cent sure-fire success. If we had done that, we would have failed completely. Instead, we asked the 'why' question time and again to as many people as we could find: we simply did not believe the answer that the advisers had given us. The real 'why' slowly emerged. The civil servants were truthful that the one thing they wanted to avoid was the risk of embarrassing the minister. That is a career-limiting move for a civil servant. And our programme would not embarrass the minister if it failed: the real embarrassment would come if it succeeded. It would show that existing government programmes were hopelessly ineffective and expensive: that really would embarrass the minister.

So we went back to the advisers. We paid lip service to the risks they identified, but really focused on how our programme would not affect or challenge any existing government programmes; instead, it would support them. And anyway, we assured them, it would be a very modest programme. The civil servants started purring with delight. We had understood their message: when they talk about the risks of failure, they mean they are really worried about the risks of success. Five years later, the programme became one of the top ten graduate recruiters in the UK and the minister was delighted with 'his' success.

The story shows why 'why' is essential, and how to ask 'why' well:

- **Keep asking the 'why' question**. Do not be satisfied with the initial answer. At best it will be superficial, at worst it will be wrong.

- **Get help**. One person can never have as much insight as a whole group. Do not be the lone hero: hunting in a pack is normally better than hunting alone.

Asking the 'why' question may not turn you into a James Bond villain who reaches the cusp of world domination. But it will help you sell better. As with all the other basic questions, to sell well you have to reach beyond the obvious answer. Keep challenging yourself. Do not accept the simple sales pack from head office as the complete answer. See the world through the eyes of your customer, not through the eyes of marketing gurus in head office. As you learn to see the world through your customers' eyes, so you will reach better answers to all the key sales questions. You will be setting yourself up to succeed.

Chapter 2

Persuasive conversations

*S*elling used to scare me. It sounded like a battle. The seller had to defeat the buyer: death or glory. I liked the glory part of that equation, but I was not quite so keen on the alternative.

It was Archie who put me right. He made a career out of selling to grocery stores in the 'nils' part of Scotland, as in the football results:

Arbroath 0, Celtic 5

Forfar Athletic 0, Hibernian 4

Montrose 0, Aberdeen 2

He was proud of his unwavering support for the unremitting failure of his football teams. Fortunately, Archie showed more judgement in his approach to selling than he did to football.

For Archie, selling is not a battle: it is a conversation. Having eight conversations a day is much better than having eight battles a day, especially if there is a risk of scoring nil at the end of the day.

A sales conversation is not like a social conversation, which can be a random walk of discovery. A sales conversation is structured and directed. It is, above all, a persuasive conversation with a clear outcome. And once you understand the underlying structure of the sales conversation, you can use it to sell anything, from nappies to multi-million-dollar contracts. I have used this structure across the world: from Japan and Asia, through the Middle East and Europe to America; in most industries and for everything from a small order in a grocery store all the way to persuading a bank board to start up a new bank. The conversation can take anything from a few seconds to a year or more, but the underlying structure does not vary.

At the heart of the persuasive conversation is the idea of 'incremental commitment'. At each stage of the conversation you are asking the client to make a very small commitment to you. It is so small, so natural, that the client hardly feels that they are making any commitment at all. The first commitment they make is to speak to you. Big commitment? No. Important commitment? Absolutely essential. By building the commitments step by step you herd the client into a place where they naturally say yes. One way of thinking about this logical flow is as a series of traffic lights: you stay at each stage of the conversation until the client's lights go green, and then you move on.

Once again, it was Archie who introduced me to the idea of incremental commitment and the logical flow of a persuasive conversation. Archie was one of nature's enthusiasts. He had a passion not just for football, but for life and for selling. He even used PASSION as the structure of his persuasive conversations. Passion was his motto. Here is what PASSION stood for:

Preparation and purpose.

Alignment and rapport.

Situation review with the client.

So what's in it for me, the client?

Idea suggested simply.

Overcome any objections.

Next steps and close.

If you remember and use this seven-step logic, you will never go too far wrong in a sales conversation. This structure has worked for selling nappies in Birmingham, consulting in Korea and selling to CEOs and to government ministers. It is a universal formula, although the way you apply it differs radically depending on context.

I would not ask a government minister to do my favourite side-by-side nappy test – unless I was suffering from career death wish.

The PASSION structure is both a logical flow and an emotional flow. If you follow the logical and emotional flow properly, you will normally arrive at a sale at the far end. Most sales guides focus only on the logical flow; that is important, but it is only half the story, at most. Just as important is to understand the emotional flow. If the customer is emotionally on board, they are much more likely to stay on board with the logic. If they fall overboard emotionally, it is more or less impossible to bring them back on board through force of logic.

A persuasive conversation is like any other sort of conversation in that it is both logical and emotional – both the subject and the person are engaged.

Managing the emotional flow

The emotional flow is about turning a series of red lights into green lights with the buyer. The buyer may start with a whole series of red lights which stand between you and the sale. These red lights are:

- Why should I talk to you: what's in it for me?
- Can I trust you?
- I am confused, but don't want to admit it: so I take no risk and make no decision.
- I feel I am being pushed into a corner.
- Who's side is he on: mine or his?
- Will I look foolish if I buy?
- What can I tell colleagues and friends if I buy?

If this is what the customer is thinking, then you will be in trouble. The chances of selling to a disengaged client are somewhere between zip and zero.

Step one is to get the client engaged and to keep them engaged. Emotionally, they should be switching all their lights to green, and this is what they should be thinking about you:

● I need to talk to you to deal with a need or opportunity I have.

● Here is someone I can trust.

● You understand my situation even better than I do: I now know what I need.

● You are helpful, expert and impartial: I am not being painted into a corner.

● You are on my side: you are helping me rather than pushing your own agenda.

● I will have no regrets about buying from you.

● I can show my colleagues and friends that I made a really smart decision.

When all the lights turn green, it takes a genius not to make the sale. So the successful sale is as much emotional as it is logical, even at the most senior levels of selling. Put bluntly, if the CEO is buying something from you (consulting services, for instance) he is putting his reputation on the line. He will think long and hard about how far he can really trust the person in front of him: promises are easy, delivery is hard. He will want to be safe in your hands. The CEO can take references, hear your pitch and interview you, but ultimately logic only goes so far. Emotion comes into it as well: he will buy into you as much as buying into what you say.

If the emotional foundations are secure, then the logical conversation can succeed. Without the foundations in place, the logic keeps on falling down into a pit of apparently illogical objections, irrational deviations and perverse non-engagement.

Managing the logical flow

We have already met PASSION. Each stage of the conversation is like a set of traffic lights, just like the emotional flow above.

We cannot go from one stage to the next until the traffic lights have turned green for us. If you try crossing the client's red lights, the carnage that ensues can be ugly. Here is what green traffic lights look like for each stage of the logical flow of the persuasive conversation:

- **Preparation and purpose**. You have done your homework on the client; you understand what the buyer needs and how they work; you have a clear goal (and back-up) for the meeting; you have prepared all the logistics and materials for the meeting.

- **Alignment and rapport**. The client has opened up, is talking freely and has no defensive body language. The client is talking more than you, and nodding when you do say anything.

- **Situation review with the client**. You understand the client's current situation and how they want to change it; you have understood the pay-off or benefits of the desired change; you have an understanding of the decision criteria they will use in buying; you have price-qualified the client.

- **So what's in it for me, the client?** You have stated, in your own words, the financial or non-financial benefits that the client desires and the client has agreed: you believe you can deliver those benefits.

- **Idea suggested simply**. You have stated your solution clearly and simply; your explanation of how it works will play to the client's hopes and fears and answer their main questions before they are asked; the client is quiet, focused and nodding in agreement.

- **Overcome any objections**. Your explanation of the idea will pre-empt most of the objections the client has; any questions the client has will mainly be to clarify and confirm rather than to challenge. The client looks relaxed and is ready to be closed.

- **Next steps and close**. Your close confirms agreement and next steps, which the client agrees to.

At each stage of the process, the client is making a very small and very modest agreement with you. At first, the client is doing no more than recognising that it is worth talking to you. Then they outline their situation and needs before agreeing with your summary of what has been said. And even after those first two, very modest, steps, they have started moving towards agreeing with you.

This incremental commitment process has some basic implications for how you use the logical flow:

● Invest time in the early stages of the conversation: this is where you make sure you get the client into the right position to agree.

● Do not jump steps: you are likely to scare the client away.

● If the client starts causing problems later in the process, it is probably because the foundations were not laid properly at the start. So go back to the situation review and rebuild: avoid getting into an argument where you may not have understood the situation properly from the client's point of view.

● The logical flow is not a script: it allows you to use your own style and to adapt to the situation as needed.

Because the logical flow is based on the idea of incremental commitment, you need to recognise the signs that the client is ready to move to the next stage of the conversation. You have to wait for the green light before proceeding.

This logical flow can look daunting. When I was first introduced to it, I was confused by it. I had so much to remember about the products, the forms I was meant to fill in, the objections I had to handle and what to do with my ever-present sales trainer, that trying to work out a new way of talking was too much. So we need to make it easy for ourselves. There are two ways we can do this. First, remember the traffic lights principle: you only need to deal with one set of traffic lights (one stage of the conversation) at a time. It is not a script: it is a guide to what you should be talking about. Second, master the logical flow one stage at a time. You do not need to master the whole logical flow instantly.

In practice, the logical flow can be very simple and very quick indeed. For instance, once I was working a team hard in Brussels. They were all highly committed over-achievers who would never work one hour when they could work twelve. There had been plenty of late nights, and I was worried they might burn out. So I thought they needed a break. So how long would it take to get them out of the office? I went into the team room in sales mode:

P My goal was to get the team out of the office, where they were doing more harm than good.

A 'It looks like we are all knackered.' Everyone nodded.

S 'We all need a break, don't we?' More nodding.

S 'Which will allow us to be fresh for the big day tomorrow.'

I 'Let's leave this and go to the bar next door.' Smiles appeared …

O 'I'll buy the first round.' Looks of disbelief all round …

N 'Last person out buys the second round.'

I was nearly killed in the stampede for the door. The pitch had lasted perhaps 25 seconds. Purists will note that I was guilty of the cardinal sin of talking, not listening. But it makes the point. The logical flow can be very simple, if you want it to be.

Having introduced PASSION, it is now time to look in detail at each stage of the logical flow.

Preparation and purpose

Having good preparation and a clear purpose for each sales call is obvious. It is so obvious that it is routinely missed and the sale is lost before it starts. The three most common mistakes are:

- **Under-preparing**. The minimum you should know before each call is:
  - Who you are calling on, who else you may meet (secretaries, colleagues, etc.) and what you might want from these people.

- What their current state of business is like, especially concerning your products and services.
- What the client needs and wants, and how they work and buy.
- What data you need to share, what materials you need and how to organise them properly.
- All the basic logistics of time, place, contact details and confirmation of the meeting.

- **Over-preparing**. Sitting behind a desk and filling in forms or staring at the internet is a wonderful substitute for work. Unlike clients, spreadsheets don't argue back. Cubicle land with its coffee machines is comfortable; if that is what you prefer, do not get into sales.

- **Not having a clear goal**. In many sales calls the goal is clear: close the sale. High-ticket and complex sales will take many calls over weeks or months: you cannot close the sale immediately. You need to break your conversation into stages and build commitment incrementally: each conversation should lead to one more action or agreement. And you should have a Plan A and a Plan B: don't put all your eggs in one basket. You cannot hope for a good outcome; you have to plan for a good outcome.

Alignment and rapport

It is easier to sell to an ally than to an adversary. Before getting into the logic of the sale, you need some degree of personal rapport. This point was made over 70 years ago by Dale Carnegie in *How to Win Friends and Influence People*. His book is corny and useful in equal amounts. The style may be dated, but the message is not. He recounts the tale of a property developer who has a big prestige project. It is about to miss its completion date because one supplier is behind schedule: if the supplier does not deliver on time, the project will slip and penalty clauses will be invoked. The property developer stands to lose a fortune. To make it worse, the property developer is only a small customer of the supplier: it really does not matter to the supplier if the property developer goes bust.

You are the property developer. What would you do?

The normal human reaction is to start working the phones and emails until they glow red-hot. Plead, bully, beg, persuade, cajole; do whatever it takes to get the supplier back on track. At worst, get in the lawyers. And the chances are that this approach would simply annoy the supplier. If lucky, you might move the delivery date forward by a week or so, but you are still out of business.

The property developer was smart. He did not think like a buyer. He thought like a salesperson: his job was to sell his needs and his priorities to the supplier, to persuade the supplier to change his priorities. So he rang the owner of the supply company and asked if he could visit the factory, and perhaps take the owner out to lunch. The owner was surprised and agreed. They toured the factory and the developer and owner talked as they walked. The owner had feared a difficult conversation, but instead his chest started to puff with pride as the developer admired what the owner had achieved in creating a successful business

Over lunch, the two of them talked more about business, about life, about a mutual interest in golf and other matters. The developer never mentioned the supply problem. Towards the end of lunch, the supplier raised the matter. The developer briefly outlined his problem. The supplier simply asked: 'So when do you need it by?'. The developer answered and the supplier immediately promised to fix his schedules to help out. Problem solved. If you want to win a battle, first win a friend. It is easier to sell to an ally than to an enemy.

> if you want to win a battle, first win a friend

Clearly, we cannot spend the best part of a day building rapport with each prospective client. We need some quicker ways of doing so. The easiest way to do this is to let people talk about their favourite subject: themselves. If you meet in their offices, there are normally plenty of cues to follow up. Framed pictures invite a question: ask about the car, house, holiday snap or diploma. Even at senior levels, where time is precious, prospective clients may well 'waste' time in idle chit-chat when they first meet. Except that the gossip has a purpose. When they chat about the industry, about their experiences, some of the people they know, they really want to see if you swim in the same pool as they do: do you know the same people, have you got shared experiences, do you really know the industry? It is like watching dogs sniffing each other out. They want to know if they can do business with you: are you credible or not?

Fortunately, most of us are dealing with buyers we already know. Even here, it pays to start the conversation with some simple rapport building. This serves two functions. First, it refreshes the relationship: it shows that you are both insiders and have an interest in working together. Second, it enables the buyer to refocus: perhaps they have had a bad meeting with the previous salesperson, or they had a row with the boss, or they are worried about a project deadline or about getting a trainer to teach their pet hamster yoga. Give the buyer the space to get rid of all that mental clutter and emotional baggage.

For every rule, there is an exception. And there are some buyers out there who regard social chat as an offence against their professional pride and precious time. They want to get straight down to business, with no nonsense: 'Tell me the facts and I'll tell you my decision.' And you can deal with them that way. But even with them, over time it pays to get past the mask they wear. I had huge trouble with Tom, who was the classic 'no-nonsense buyer', so one day I saw him and the conversation started like this:

'Right Tom, I have the best deal for you since Godzilla met King Kong.'

'Godzilla never met King Kong', replied Tom testily.

'Precisely, that's how good the deal is ...'

'You mean, it's complete rubbish.'

'Judge for yourself, here it is ....' I said, and went straight into the pitch Tom required.

By now Tom was keen to see just how bad the deal was. Instead of criticising me for the deal not being great, he criticised it for not being as bad as I had claimed. And so he bought the deal, just to prove me wrong. Sale made, thanks to using the contradiction principle, which we cover later on. More important, it set up a running joke: every time he met me he would ask how bad my deal was this time, and I would give him another creative reply. Slowly, Tom the buyer morphed into Tom the human being. Sales steadily rose, month on month.

Situation review with the client

Once the client has relaxed and is ready to engage, the next step is to review and understand the client's situation, from their perspective. That means lots of listening, little talking and a few good questions.

'What is the capital of Croatia?'

'42.'

'42' is potentially a very good answer to many questions, such as 'What is 7 multiplied by 6?' For fans of Douglas Adams novels, it is also the ultimate answer to 'What is the meaning of life?' But it is a lousy answer to the question 'What is the capital of Croatia?' If you don't know the question, you can't know the answer. If you do not know the client's problem or opportunity, you cannot know what to sell to them.

Weak salesmen are 42ers: they have one answer to everything and that is what they push, regardless of what the client needs or wants. Strong salespeople may only have one product (their '42') but they are smart enough to work out the client's situation first. Once they see the world through the eyes of the client, they can work out how '42' fits into the client's landscape.

Reviewing the situation is the first step to making sure we understand the client's needs. It is a way of qualifying the client around needs, scope and price. Only when you have understood the facts can you hope to draw out the implications, understand the pay-off and start presenting your idea in the context of what the client really wants.

Some of the fact gathering should already have happened before you even meet the client. You should know all the basics about the firm, the client's title and their position. Asking these sorts of questions will not help you: they will display your ignorance and waste the client's time. Marshal the basic facts in advance. Focus your questions on a few key areas:

- Key facts you cannot reasonably be expected to know in advance.
- How the current situation is working.
- What the client need or problem is.
- What criteria the client will use for deciding between options.
- What budget the client has: qualify on value and price as early as possible.

For instance, if you are selling photocopiers to a company that is currently a client of your competitor, you will probably want to ask the following sorts of questions:

- **Key facts you cannot reasonably be expected to know in advance**. Ask 'What are your current copy requirements (volume, colour, etc.)?'
- **How the current situation is working**. Ask 'What's good about your existing arrangements?' 'What would you like to

improve or change?' Avoid 'What's wrong?': it implies the client made a bad decision last time. Instead, remain positive; find out what the client likes as well as what the client dislikes.

● **What the client need or problem is**. Link the situation to a problem and an outcome: 'How often do you experience copier down time, for how long and what impact does that have?' 'How often do you need specialist copy jobs that have to be outsourced – and how convenient is that?'

● **What criteria the client will use for deciding between options**. Ask this directly: 'What are the top two to three criteria you will use in making your decision?' They always say 'price', so probe: initial price, cost per month, cost per sheet, cost versus reliability (hidden costs of downtime, etc.).

● **Qualify on value and price**. Value is simply benefits less price. So before price-qualifying, value-qualify. Establish the potential scale of benefits from moving to a faster, more reliable or higher quality copier. Price only makes sense in the context of the value it can deliver. The simple approach is often best: 'What is your expected budget for this?' You can also ask this indirectly: 'Are you expecting to spend more or less on copying in future?' If you know what they already have, you should be able to estimate their current costs. Price qualification is an art form in its own right and is covered later. In general, the earlier you qualify the better: it avoids tears later on. But qualification needs to be done in such a way that it does not put the client on the defensive.

As the customer talks, they will be giving you your sales script. They will be telling you what they want and why they want it. All you have to do next is to replay that information back to them, showing how your product meets their stated needs. At this stage, focus on hot buttons: these are the buttons you need to push to make the customer buy. Hot buttons are typically the customer's biggest hopes and fears:

- This is what I really like and want.
- This is what makes me mad as hell.

Typically, clients will not be able to tell you precisely what they want. You have to act like a doctor at this stage in the conversation: listen carefully to all the slightly garbled symptoms which the client is complaining about, then probe to find out what the real problem, need or opportunity is.

Up to this point, the client should have been doing about 80 per cent of the talking, and you should have done all the listening. Once you are confident that you have the customer's hot buttons, you understand their hopes and fears and you have all the relevant facts about what they need and how they will decide, you can move on to the next stage.

So what's in it for me, the client?

Answering the 'So what' question is central to success. Some people call it the WIFM point: 'What's in it for me?' When you answer the question well, you have value-qualified the client. Value qualification is as important as price qualification. If you ask someone 'Do you want to spend £1,000?' the answer will either be 'No' or 'On what?': you cannot price-qualify unless you have also value-qualified. If you have established that the value the client seeks is worth £2,000, then price-qualifying them for £1,000 is simple.

Step one: move from facts to conclusions

The first step in answering the 'So what' question is to move from gathering facts to drawing conclusions. Start by paraphrasing back to the client what they have told you:

- So if I have understood correctly, you want a desk-top computer that edits videos, plays high-end games and costs less than £750 all in?

- So you need to integrate these six computer systems and achieve a 30 per cent cost reduction with a potential to scale up 100 per cent with no quality loss. And you need to complete in two years?

- So you want a new logo that builds on your existing heritage, but makes it more dynamic. It must be easily recognisable across the globe and offend no one?

To make it slightly more informal and less threatening, I often dress this up a little:

- So the exam question you are setting me is: can I find a computer that ...?

- So the challenge for me is to find you a computer that ...?

Clients like this approach. I am not pushing a solution on them, which might make them feel like they are losing control. Instead, they are setting me the problem; they are handing their problem over to me. That does not threaten them; it makes them feel good about the way the conversation is going. And at this stage, a pause helps. Pause and quietly shake your head or stroke your chin; do something to show that you are really having to think about the client's needs. Avoid the temptation to rush to a snap solution: it will not look authentic. It will sound like 'This is what I prepared before and was always going to offer you anyway'. The more you are seen to be thinking about how to respond, the more it will look like you are responding to their needs, not simply pushing your pre-packed solution.

Do not rush to the solution. First, gain agreement from the client that you have got the right problem or opportunity. You are doing a soft close around the opportunity statement. The clearest way of gaining agreement is to ask for it. This is the direct close, and it works best where the client has come to you with a question. This might be the computer

> the clearest way of gaining agreement is to ask for it

buyer in a retail store or the CEO who is looking for consulting advice for a major change programme. In each case they have a need, and they want to hear that you have understood it correctly. So ask them directly whether they agree with your summary:

- Is that the correct exam question?
- Have I summarised your expectations correctly?
- Is that the challenge you want to address?

If the client sounds uncertain, keep probing until you get a clear yes from them. Don't push them or force them into agreement: it will not last long enough to make the sale. The chances are that you may have not fully understood their situation. So go back one step and ask some more open questions:

- What else are you looking at?
- What are the most important outcomes you want?
- What do you want to change?

Where you have approached the client, a different dynamic is at work. You might be selling life assurance, or approaching a senior executive with a new idea that could improve their business. You still need to gain the agreement of the executive that you are talking about something worthwhile. Again, the direct close is often most powerful at this stage of the conversation:

- Is reducing staff turnover a priority for you?
- Would you like to reduce inventory/increase speed to market?
- Would you like to provide properly for your retirement – and for your widow?

The difference is that you are gaining their agreement to an opportunity or problem you have suggested, not to a problem or opportunity the client has suggested. Either way, get the client to agree that it is a worthwhile opportunity to work on.

If this stage of the conversation is done well, it will last a few seconds. The time is small but the commitment is huge. Once the client has committed to the agreed problem or opportunity, they are swimming firmly towards your net. Now you just have to keep them swimming in the same direction – and don't drop the net.

Step two: move from conclusions to benefits to the client

This is another short but important step. It reinforces the agreement you have just made. Here is why it is important: human nature.

Human nature is very risk-averse. That is probably because our ancestors lived in constant fear of being eaten by a mammoth and we are in constant fear of being eaten by our boss. Look at what happens when someone has a bright idea in a meeting: everyone else around the table gets out their heat-seeking missiles and shoots the idea down. This shows that they are very clever, because they have identified all the risks that any new idea has. No one starts exploring why the idea might actually be a good idea. By the time all the heat-seeking missiles have hit the idea, it has been destroyed. It might have been an outstanding idea, worth all the risk. But it is easier to be negative and cautious than positive and optimistic. Unless, of course, you work in sales. Salespeople are the antidote to corporate life. We are one of the few sources of energy, enthusiasm and positive thinking. Buyers, inevitably, are among the most risk-averse and negative people of the corporate tribe.

If you suggest your idea too early, the negative buyer will dip into a back pocket, get out some heat-seeking missiles and start firing. You can prevent that game by exploring all the benefits of finding the solution before you explain your idea in detail. By the time the buyer has thought about the cornucopia of wonderful benefits that might come their way, they are more likely to regard your suggestion positively when you finally deliver it.

There are three ways of reinforcing the benefits with the client:

- Tell the client.
- What we find.
- Ask the client.

Tell the client

This has the virtue of being direct and the vice of not being credible: it may sound like empty boasting. But if you know that these are the benefits the client wants, and you can deliver them, then go direct. Don't mess around.

Imagine you are selling a car to a fitness coach who spends most of her time on the road visiting different clients. She has an old clunker to which she is emotionally attached, but it is unreliable. She is thinking of trading up but is worried that it may simply be an extravagant waste of money. So what are the potential benefits of trading up for the fitness coach?

- **Reliability**. Less time off the road means less lost revenues.
- **Image**. If you look cheap, you charge cheap. If you want higher rates, look the part.
- **Comfort**. If you arrive less tired, you can do better work and retain more clients.
- **GPS**. Less time spent getting lost means more time earning money.
- **Safety**. She is less likely to have an accident in the new car (which has an anti-lock braking system) and less likely to be injured (air bags and crumple zones), which means less risk of lost earnings.
- **Security**. Automatic locking and other features mean that there is less risk of the car being stolen (which would mean time off the road and lost revenues). And the safety and security features also mean lower outgoings in terms of insurance.

If your fitness coach has already told you that these are the benefits she is looking for, then you will not go far wrong in summarising them. If she has simply told you that she wants 'reliability, image, comfort, safety and a GPS system', then the other benefits may not sound credible.

This approach allows you to reinforce the benefits (value) of the purchase: the new car ceases to be an extravagance and it becomes an investment that she can justify. The problem with this approach is that it can sound theoretical rather than practical. And if you try to pin a specific monetary value on the amount of down-time avoided, you will probably not be credible: you will not know enough about her situation and you are dealing with the possibility, not reality, of down-time. So you need a way of making all the benefits of the new car sound credible and compelling. This is where the 'what we find' approach often works well.

What we find

This is one of the most powerful ways I have come across of seeding ideas into a buyer's head. Instead of boasting about how wonderful our offering is, get a client to do it for you. Use the credibility of other clients who are similar to the person in front of you who is thinking of buying. Use peer group pressure to influence the buyer. If all the peers of the buyer are thinking or doing something, the buyer will find it hard to go in the opposite direction of the herd. If you say that

> use peer group pressure to influence the buyer

the new car for the fitness coach will save her money, it will be hard for you to back that claim up in any detail. But if she hears of a real-life example of other people making the same decision, the money-saving claim suddenly becomes much more credible.

'What we find' is simply a story that starts with 'What we find other clients tell us is ...'

In the case of the fitness coach you may not have had a swarm of female fitness coaches coming to the dealership looking to trade up. But you will have come across plenty of other professionals and self-employed people who are in the same situation: they depend on their car for their trade.

'We had a freelance journalist (or IT consultant, or photographer, etc.) come here last month. He traded up. What he told us was that:

- reliability meant he spent less time off the road, and he lost fewer revenue hours;
- with the better image he projected (together with a new suit) he was able to increase his rates by 15 per cent;
- the safety and security features of this car meant that he was able to reduce his insurance premiums;
- he also said he was able to start and finish the day much less tired than before ...'

You are making the same benefits claims as before, but with much more power and credibility.

The same 'what we find' can be used with CEOs. So if you are selling a new IT system, you can say how brilliant it is. Boasting to a CEO about your brilliant service simply invites push-back and denial: they will tell you that their situation is different, they have different needs or they will simply get into an argument about the details of how your claim stacks up. The better alternative is to use a 'what we find' and tell the CEO 'What we find is that other clients who have implemented this system typically achieve 25 per cent cost savings and a payback on the initial investment of just over two years. In particular, one client told us ...' The 'what we find' approach invites curiosity, not hostility. CEOs and senior executives are always keen to know what other firms are doing: they do not want to be left behind. They may argue against your claims, but they will not argue against another firm's experience.

Telling a story has power at several levels:

- It uses the credibility of other clients on your behalf.
- It is harder to deny the experience of other clients than it is to deny your claims.
- Clients tend to imagine into the story what they want to hear, while ignoring the parts of the story that do not apply to them.
- The story invites more questions and elicits a warmer response than arguing over directly claimed benefits.

The more specific your 'what we find' is, the more credible it becomes. Vague statements are rarely believed, and rightly so. They do not sound authentic and they probably are not. A story that is rich in detail is hard to make up, and is more likely to be truthful.

Ask the client

The most credible way of establishing the benefits is to ask the client. Usually, people do not argue against their own ideas – not even buyers. Once they have stated the true benefits of what they are looking for, they will be hungry to see those benefits delivered. They will be swimming vigorously towards your sales net.

Typically, clients are mushy when talking about desired benefits. They find it hard to articulate what they really want. So the IT fitness coach buying the car talks about 'comfort, reliability, image and GPS'. This is where you have to probe with some open but directed questions:

- How will reliability affect your business?
- Why is image so important?
- How will comfort help you?

It is possible that a nightmare story will come out which shows why the purchase is absolutely compelling. Perhaps she was embarrassed when she lost a key client by missing a training session because the car broke down. These are far more compelling reasons to buy than vague statements about image and reliability.

Idea suggested simply

Each stage of a persuasive conversation gets easier and easier. The early stages of the conversation are the hardest: getting the client heading in the right direction is the tough part of the conversation. Suggest the idea must be kept short and simple. The longer it is, the greater the risk of overselling. The more you tell people about your wonderful idea, the greater the risk. You may raise points that trouble the client or they had not even thought about. Success is not when you have said everything there is to be said; it is when you have said the least that needs to be said. Less is more. So what is the minimum? There are at most three items to cover here:

- **State the idea**. This can be one sentence: 'Based on what you say, this car/copier/computer/project looks like it fits your needs best.'

- **State why it is the best-fit idea**. This reinforces the client's desired benefits again, but now relates them to the specific performance characteristics of your suggestion: 'You want great fuel economy: this car does 60 mpg, which is best in class.'

- **If necessary, explain the details of how it works**. This can be used as an opportunity to pre-empt some objections (see next section). In more complex sales, such as consulting engagements, this is a chance to let the client co-create the detailed design with you. In complex selling, this is where you move from 'push' selling to consultative selling: giving the client ownership over what they are going to buy.

Provided the customer still has a pulse, you should get a reaction to your suggestion. The traffic lights should show red, amber or green. Each reaction is obvious. Normally it will be stated. It may be signalled with body language: from smiling, touching the product and relaxing, through to tensing up, retreating, or shaking the head. You do not need to be a world expert at body language to see if the client is engaging: you simply need to be observant.

- **Green light**. If your groundwork has been good, the client will be ready to buy now. Never stop your client buying. Don't oversell. Close right now (see the section after next on closing).

- **Amber light**. This is where the client is non-committal. They may well have one or two unspoken concerns or objections. The first task is to qualify those objections: move to the next section (on handling objections).

- **Red light**. If a red light is flashing, do not proceed: the resulting sales crash could be messy. First, check the nature of the red light. It may simply be a misunderstanding: in one case I got push-back because the client thought I had quoted in pounds but I had quoted in dollars: that was a $3 million misunderstanding. As soon as the currency was clear, the client was so relieved he agreed immediately in principle. If the red light is more substantive, do not simply stop: go into reverse. Go back a step and make sure that you have properly understood the client's situation and needs.

Overcome any objections

Prevention is always better than cure. The best way to handle objections is to pre-empt them. Ideally, you will have pre-empted all the buyers' objections when you explained how the idea worked: the client should be ready for the close. But life is rarely as simple as that. Clients like to show that they are alive by asking questions. The challenge is to know what sort of questions you are getting and how to deal with them. Typically, four types of reaction emerge at this point:

- aggressive and negative;
- passive or evasive;
- inquisitive;
- positive.

How you respond depends on the nature of the reaction. Here is how to deal with each type of response.

Aggressive and negative buyer reaction

This is the reaction that is often feared, but it should not be. It is where the client turns round in anger or disbelief and says things like:

- That costs far too much.
- There is no way we need that size order.
- Have you done your homework? If you knew anything about us you would realise that is impossible.
- Have you lost leave of your senses?
- Have you any idea what you are talking about?

I first discovered the full power of the aggressive and negative reaction when I was dealing with a Co-op store manager. I had done my stock check and ran through a suggested order with him. Halfway through he stopped me and asked, in a heavy Scottish accent, if I would like a 'bunch of feuves'. I had never heard of 'feuves' before, but the way he was holding his fist in my face suggested that 'feuves' was Scottish for the five knuckles on his hand. I figured out that perhaps he was not entirely comfortable with the order I was suggesting. To handle his objection, I pointed at my very broken nose and invited him to imagine what had happened to the person who did it to me. I then said I would check the stock again and left the store in stunned silence. Five minutes later I returned. The store manager offered me a cup of tea and we became the unlikeliest of friends. This is not an approach that I would recommend normally. But it draws out the good news about the negative and aggressive response: at least the client is engaged. Once the client is engaged in what you are suggesting, you can start to work towards a solution.

> once the client is engaged, you can start to work towards a solution

The good news about the very hostile reaction, where the client may be shouting, is that most people find such hostility very hard to sustain. It is physically and emotionally exhausting. As an exercise, I sometimes ask groups to see how long they can keep a diatribe going at full volume. Most people give up within two minutes, which can seem like an eternity if you are on the receiving end of it. But provided you do not add any fuel to the fire by arguing back, you will find that the client's anger burns itself out fairly fast, and you can slowly get back to a rational discussion.

There are three ways to respond to the aggressive and negative reaction:

- aggressive;
- passive;
- assertive.

- **The aggressive reaction**. This is fighting fire with fire: it is all about win/lose, 'me first', and there is a fair amount of pride and ego involved. In at least 99 per cent of cases it is not a smart reaction. It simply inflames the situation. The argument gets worse, not better. As a rule, never argue with babies, taxi drivers or God: even if you are right it does you no good. To that list, you can add buyers: there is no point in winning the argument and losing the order. Not only do you lose the order, you lose a friend – and you lose the prospect of further orders. The 1 per cent of time when it pays to fight back is when you have little to lose and much to gain by fighting hard.

- **The passive reaction**. This is the classic victim mindset: 'Poor me: I am a victim of a cruel world which I cannot change.' This is a mindset that should be completely alien to a salesperson. Under stress, it can be tempting to wave the white flag and give up. This is another version of win/lose, in which the victim caves in and becomes a doormat for the aggressor. Clearly, there are limits to how far you should push. For instance, once I was gathering support for a parliamentary election: selling politics. I went to pick up a supporter and rang on his door. I asked the lady who answered if Mr Jones would be voting today. The lady wept a little and said no. I asked why not. 'He died a couple of minutes ago', she said. A more resolute salesperson might have put the body in a wheelchair and wheeled it down to the polling station. I failed the sales test, although perhaps I passed the humanity test, by helping her out instead.

- **The assertive reaction.** This is the ideal reaction. Be clear about your interests and positions, and seek clarity about the client's interests and positions. The sort of language that is assertive but not aggressive includes classic paraphrasing and listening questions:

  - If I have understood correctly, you are saying that your main interest is ... your main objections are ... and your most important expectations are ...?

  - When you say it costs too much, what are you judging the cost against [initial cost, lifetime cost, cost per use, cost compared to competition ...]?

  - What points have I missed in this proposal?

  - What else do you need to know to make a decision?

The aggressor will often use personal and emotive language: it is a common abuse that is best ignored. As soon as you rise to the bait of provocation, you have lost: they will get on their high horse and tell you that you are not professional and will threaten you with complaints and more. And buyers can be the worst of the lot. Ignore the provocation and emotion: focus on the facts. If you have got some of the facts plain wrong, do not try to argue your way out of it: avoiding the truth makes you sound untrustworthy or, worse, like a politician. If you have messed up, recognise the error. 'Sorry' may be the hardest word to say, but it will draw the sting out of the conversation. At all stages the goal is to get away from an irrational conversation to a conversation based on facts, interests, needs and wants. The longer you stick to the rational conversation, without sinking into an emotional tit for tat, the harder the buyer finds it to sustain their position.

Passive or evasive buyer reaction

Sales is the natural habitat of optimists: as a rule optimism is vital to survival and success. As ever, there is an exception to every rule, and this is it: when buyers are passive or evasive, wishful thinking can take the salesperson over. We may interpret the lack of outright opposition as tacit agreement. We then get to the end of an increasingly one-sided pitch, go for the close and get a rejection. If buyers are interested in buying, they are rarely passive: they normally are actively engaged. They will show active engagement in a whole number of ways:

- asking questions;
- challenging what you say;
- nodding agreement;
- leaning forward into your space;
- playing with a sample;
- picking up the product.

The more of these behaviours the buyer shows, the more actively engaged they are. If they show none of these engagement signals, then there is no reason to assume that they are engaging. If they do not engage, they do not buy. Classic evasive behaviour includes:

- difficulty in getting a meeting scheduled;
- arriving late for a meeting or rescheduling it;
- looking at their watch during a meeting;
- being distracted by other calls/texts during the meeting;
- looking away/over your shoulder;
- fidgeting.

If this is the sort of reaction you are getting, there is a simple reason: you have not found their problem, need or opportunity. You may be excited about your product; they are not. You may be able to offer them a £1 million cost saving every year, but you are speaking to the wrong person in the company: it may be the company's problem, but it is not that manager's problem.

The solution is to stop. Do not try to stir up apathy. Go back to a review of the situation, to understand the buyer's real needs and interests and to find a problem or opportunity that genuinely engages them. Put simply, when in a hole, stop digging. The passive reaction is a deeper and more deadly hole than the aggressive reaction.

Inquisitive buyer reaction

Clients ask questions for all sorts of reasons:

- They are bored of listening and want to say something.
- They want to look clever by asking a smart question.
- They have a form to fill in and a procedure to follow.
- They think that they ought to ask a question.
- They have a real question which needs a real answer.

In other words, many questions are about ritual, not substance. This is especially true in public sector procurement, where vast swathes of irrelevant and useless information is required. Well, not entirely irrelevant. The questions give some low-level bureaucrats a reason to exist and an excuse for some meetings, which beat real work any day of the week. Humour them as you should humour all such ritual questions. Short answers are better than long answers. Answering the questions does not progress the sale. Not answering them will result in the whole sales process falling down, if only because you have insulted the dignity of the person asking the question and you have not been able to tick every box.

> short answers are better than long answers

The key virtue in dealing with ritual questions is patience: it can be a marathon contest in which the last person standing wins: they should run out of questions before you run out of answers.

For fans of Monty Python, it is a real-life version of the Cheese Shop sketch. The process I was taught by one experienced and successful salesperson is inelegantly called 'grinf***ing the buyer'. Grin and bear it for as long as you can. What you think behind your grin is for you alone.

Aside from the ritual and bureaucratic questions, buyers will have genuine and legitimate questions. These present a wonderful opportunity to build and strengthen the sale. Typical constructive questions are in the form of 'How does this work for me?'

That is an invitation to have a deeper dialogue about what the client really needs, and what is unique about their context and requirements.

Dealing with genuine questions requires a change of mindset. Do not think of selling. Do not think of 'overcoming objections'. Think of yourself as a partner to the client. You are there to help them solve their problems. Their questions are an ideal opportunity for you to:

- demonstrate expertise;
- build trust, by showing you are helping them solve their problems;
- create a partnership, not a buyer–vendor relationship;
- understand their situation better;
- help the client build some ownership over the final solution in more complex sales;
- enrich your sales offering in response to emerging client needs and interests.

This is true if you are selling a home computer to a family or a major IT programme to a large corporation. If you can use the questions to build trust, build knowledge and build a partnership, you are moving towards a successful close.

Positive buyer reaction

One day I found myself selling the most valuable commodity on the planet. I was selling myself. As salespeople, we should all be able to sell ourselves. I was ushered into a room with the interviewer. He was a manic Italian. As I went in he was shouting down the telephone to a client in Italian. Although the client was over 1,000 miles away, the Italian was still using extravagant hand gestures to make his point clear. Eventually he slammed the phone down and turned his attention to me:

'You ... you must be Jo!' he exclaimed.

'Yes', I replied.

'Do you speak any languages?'

'Only English.'

'I like you. You're honest!'

'Good, so will you hire me then?'

'Of course!'

And that was the end of the interview. I started work a few weeks later. It probably was not a model in terms of interview techniques, although the result was pretty good for everyone. But from a sales perspective it illustrates one key point: never oversell. When a customer wants to buy, let them buy.

If the client is positive, don't oversell. Close fast. The more you say, the more likely you are to unsell your proposition. Overselling leads to unselling: you lose the deal that was there for the taking. The manic Italian interviewer might well have changed his mind if he had chosen to interview me for a few more minutes: later experience showed he could be volatile and unpredictable.

> the more you say, the more likely you are to unsell

If overselling does not lead to unselling, it can often lead to over-promising. It is a trick I often use as a buyer to get salespeople to over-commit and over-promise. For instance, we were reviewing some design agencies who were pitching for a fixed-price design contract; we knew our budget and simply wanted to see how much we could get for our very limited pot of money. The magic phrase I threw in halfway through one pitch was: 'I like this conversation. It is a very good conversation. I never realised you could do all this ...'

The salesperson puffed up with pride and started promising much more. So then I threw in the next provocation to overselling: the invited contradiction: 'This is great, but I bet you couldn't also do this and that ...?'

By now the salesperson was so enthusiastic, he was promising more or less everything and was determined to show he could deliver it. He won the contract and it was probably the most unprofitable piece of work his firm ever did. As a buyer it is remarkably easy to invite overselling. As a salesperson, avoid the trap. If the client is genuinely positive, move to closure fast. To check that a person is ready for closure, one simple question often helps: 'Is there anything else you want to know?'

The client is ready for the close if:

● They are positive about what you are proposing.
● They have been price-qualified.
● They have nothing more they want to ask.

When these three conditions are in place, stop selling and start closing.

Next steps and close

In golf you 'drive for show and putt for dough': a good drive looks great, but the game is more often won and lost on the less spectacular art of putting. In selling we can say that you 'present for show and close for dough'. A great sales presentation may impress, but it is the close that gets the sale. You have to close well.

A persuasive conversation is a structured conversation with a purpose. It has a beginning, a middle and an end. The close is the end, and it should be a happy ending for the client and for you. Most clients, however, are not psychic and do not know how they are meant to close the conversation for you. You have to do it for them. So you have to close, and you have to close at the right time. This is a delicate art – you can be too early or too late:

● **Close too early**. Once a prospect has said no they find it very hard to do a U-turn without losing face. An early close can turn a good prospect into an impossible one.
● **Close too late**. The conversation drifts; the more it drifts, the more time you give for risks, fears, uncertainties and doubt to emerge. In other words, you will unsell a sale that could have been made.

As you go through the sales process, keep a mental check of where the client is in terms of readiness to close. The three key questions to ask are:

- **Is the client positive about what you are proposing?** Do they understand what you are proposing? Are they making supportive comments and asking supportive questions? Does their body language show they are engaged and interested?
- **Are they price and value-qualified?** Do they have anything more to ask? Will your proposal create any surprises to them?
- **Are you speaking to the right buyer?**

No matter where you are in the logic of the conversation, if the client is ready for the close, then close. Never oversell. Clients normally give strong signals that they are ready to close. They will start asking questions that show that they have made the decision; they now simply want to know how the decision works in practice. For instance:

- Will this machine work with the one I already have?
- Can you dispose of my old machine when you install this one?
- What is the delivery schedule?
- Is payment up front, or are monthly instalments possible?
- Do you have this in blue?

The other set of close cues are non-verbal. Good signs are when the client is:

- playing with the product or sample;
- leaning forward;
- smiling or at least relaxing.

With practice, you can create hundreds of closing phrases and questions. In practice, there are four main types of close. It is worth being able to use all four:

- **The direct close**: 'Would you like to buy the car?'
- **The alternate close**: 'Would you like to buy the blue or black car?'
- **The action close**: 'Here are the keys, and if you sign here, you can drive the car off right away.'
- **The assumed close**: 'So we have all agreed that we will buy a fleet of vans with pink and green stripes.'

This section looks at each of the four main types of close and how they can be used in practice.

The direct close

This is the simplest and most powerful sort of close. It is also the most dangerous. You ask a direct question:

- Do you want to buy this?
- Do you want to go ahead?

The good news is that this is very clear, unambiguous and direct. If the answer is yes, then all is well and good. But the direct close opens up an unwelcome choice: you are asking the customer to answer yes or no. And once they have said no, they are unlikely to change their mind.

The direct close is best used when you know what the reply will be. If you know the reply will be yes, go for the direct close. Often, however, you need to give the client a little nudge to make them say the right thing. The little nudge can be one of the other closes.

The alternate close

The alternate close is sneaky but effective. You give the client a choice, but it is a restricted choice. Alternate closes sound like this:

- Would you like to pay by instalments or would you prefer to make a single payment?
- Do you want to buy the premium or the standard model?

- Would you like us to start work in two months or three months?
- Do you want this with the protection insurance or without it?

You give the client a choice about what they want to buy, but you do not give them a choice about whether they want to buy. It takes a strong client to say 'Well, actually, I don't want anything thank you'. The path of least resistance for them is to agree to one of the two choices you give them. And most people will, like water, follow the course of least resistance. It takes effort to swim against the stream. Even if the client has been dreaming up some minor questions (which they may ask later anyway), you give them the excuse to make up their mind.

The alternate close also works because it follows the principle of restricted choice. The more choice you give people, the more confused they become; when they are confused, the path of least resistance is to make no decision at all. Making no decision avoids the risk of making a mistake from the client's point of view. A limited choice is an easy choice. Ask anyone to choose between two options, and most people will find it easy to decide which of the two is better for them. Give them a choice between a thousand options and the fog of confusion will descend. Less choice is better than more.

> the more choice you give people, the more confused they become

The action close

The action close is powerful, but once in a while leads to disaster. Like the direct close, when it works it works very well. But if it fails, then the buyer will be turned off completely. They will take a stand in public, in front of you, which they will find difficult to reverse without losing face. The harder you try to recover the situation, the more they will resist, even if the resistance is irrational. They simply will not want to do a U-turn.

The action close is, as it name suggests, about using action to close the sale:

> 'Great choice: here are the car keys for you; let's sort out the paperwork and then you can drive the car away.'
>
> 'Er ... actually I don't want this car ...'

Only use the action close when you know you will gain agreement.

The assumed close

In its simplest form, the assumed close is the chairman's close. At the end of the meeting, the chairman sums up the discussion and the next steps. It takes a brave person to disagree at this stage of proceedings.

In practice, the assumed close is very effective in more complex sales where there are many people whose agreement is needed. For a sale to a big firm you may need the agreement of finance, HR and health and safety, as well as the users of your service and the power brokers who will finally approve the purchase. If you ask each person whether or not they agree, you will rapidly go nowhere. When you ask for agreement, you invite disagreement. In large firms, people prefer to say no rather than yes: no is the safer choice. And asking for agreement sounds artificial: colleagues do not seek formal approval from each other. They rely on informal consensus and mutual understanding. This is where the assumed close works.

At the end of a good meeting, I will go for an assumed close by asking my client for help with the next stage of the process: 'Thank you very much for your time: that has been a very helpful discussion. I am due to be seeing Jim next about this – have you any advice on how I can make that discussion as productive as this one?'

This formula may yield good advice on how to handle Jim. Even if they have no insight, they are flattered to be asked and they normally do not question the assumption that they have bought into what you are proposing. Ideally, the assumed close gets the client's commitment or involvement in the next stage of the process: you need a positive signal that they support you. In the best of worlds, turn your buyer into your coach. Make them into your ally, guiding you through the rest of the sales process. Other ways you can do this include:

- Who else do we need to gain support from for this proposal?
- Who would you approach next?
- What is the best way to pitch this to finance?

In sales, as in life, assumptions are deadly. The assumed close is not about assuming the buyer has bought. The only safe assumption to make is that the buyer has not bought – until they show some signs of positive commitment. The assumed close is an elegant way of helping the client show commitment.

Chapter 3

The principles and mindset of success

ood selling is not about learning a script or learning ten fancy ways to close a sale. When people talk from a script they do not sound authentic. To succeed, we need more than the tools and techniques of selling: we need the mindset of success. Fortunately, the success mindset can be learned. You do not have to inherit the right DNA to succeed. Success requires making the most of who you are.

In this chapter we will look at the principles that lie behind raising your performance. Any one of these principles can help. For instance, just learning the simple principle of 'raising the bar' (principle 5) will direct your efforts to the right place for raising sales immediately. Mastering all of the principles takes a lifetime, and I am still learning. The ten main principles of success are:

1 Trust.

2 First impressions.

3 Partner not vendor.

4 Love your client.

5 Raising the bar.

6 Learning to succeed.

7 Positive outlook.

8 High aspirations: focus on outcomes.

9 Escape the comfort zone.

10 Take control.

Trust

Let's make this simple: would you want to buy from someone you do not trust? Naturally, we all think we are fine and trustworthy people, but how is our customer to know that? The bigger the sale, the greater the risk and the more important trust becomes. I will happily buy a newspaper from a street vendor who I do not know; I will take more care over choosing a car, a builder or a dentist.

The first rule of building trust is never say 'Trust me' or its equivalents like 'To be honest with you' and 'Would I lie to you?' To see how badly this works, listen to British Prime Minister Tony Blair discussing the Iraq invasion on radio: 'Look, OK, John, I'm a straight kind of guy … Of course, I'm an honest sort of bloke – If I were lying …' (BBC Radio 4, 4 May 2005). As soon as you start proclaiming your honesty, you sound like a politician.

Instead of claiming trust, you have to build trust. Trust must be earned.

Trust is a small word with big meaning. First, let's see what trust really means, and then we will explore some strategies for building trust fast.

Trust is the product of three variables:

- values (what I say);
- credibility (what I do and who I am);
- risk.

It can be written as a formula:

$$T = \frac{(V \times C)}{R}$$

To put this into words, trust (T) is the product of my values (V: what I say) multiplied by my credibility (C: what I do and who I am), divided by the risk (R) of the situation. The bigger the transaction, the greater the risk.

Looked at this way, it becomes obvious what we have to do to build trust: we have to show that we have common interests and values with our customer. We have to back our words up with our actions. And we have to reduce the perceived risk of the transaction.

Values

Shared values are about shared interests. This is obvious and routinely missed. The classic sales pitch is based on the idea of pushing an idea on to a potential buyer. That is the opposite of sharing common interests: it is about opposition, which leads to a win/lose outcome. It pays to share the professional, and often the personal, interests of the potential client.

The quickest way to show that you share the interests of your client is to listen. Find out what they want. Be supportive and interested in what they say and what they want. The more you support what they say, the more they will think that you are on their side: they will start to trust you. You do not have to say 'Trust me'. Listening says 'Trust me' for you.

In sales, it helps to show that you are a human being. Clients like to deal with the same species as themselves. In particular, they want to deal with human beings like themselves; people trust themselves and trust people like themselves. If you can show you have common personal interests with your client, the relationship and the trust deepens fast. But you can only show that you have common interests if you know what the personal interests

> in sales, it helps to show that you are a human being

of the client are. Once again, listening helps. But for the most part, clients do not disclose much about themselves to strangers, let alone to salespeople.

In practice, if you know who you will be calling on, it is possible to find out a lot about them before you even meet. With the advent of social media you may even find that you have some friends or contacts that you share in common. If this draws a blank, then offices are often a giveaway. Managers like to personalise their space: as they do so, they will be advertising their personal lives. Pictures of vintage cars, old houses, football teams and countryside have all produced wonderful ice-breakers when meeting new prospective clients. But tread carefully if there are pictures of their wonderful and perfect family: while some managers are happy to talk about their kids to strangers, many feel it is too much of an intrusion into their personal space.

Credibility

Ultimately, credibility comes from what you do, not from what you say. This give rise to a golden rule for selling: always deliver. Always, always deliver. If you find yourself having to make excuses, you are losing credibility and trust fast: excuses are the rust in trust.

If you must always deliver, that means always setting expectations very clearly. Never over-promise just to get the sale. Curiously, having the difficult conversation about expectations can build trust and win the sale. For instance, we were pitching for a piece of work with a bank in Tokyo. The client liked what we offered but did not like the price. They wanted to do it for 40 per cent less, and said that our competitors had offered to do it for 40 per cent less. We talked through exactly what would happen if we cut the price 40 per cent. The result would be 40 per cent less cost and 100 per cent less impact, and we made it clear we would not do the work unless we could deliver a meaningful result to the client. The client had not expected this. After they chose us, they told us why: 'Because you were the only people who were honest about what could and could not be done – you saved us from wasting our money on a project which would have failed.'

Have the difficult conversation early, not late: set expectations well, rather than make excuses later.

In many cases, the credibility challenge can be dealt with even before you open your mouth. Your business card, your company name, your website, your advertising or the way you have been introduced should do most of the hard work for you. Some simple examples:

- My local plumber proudly advertises, on his van, that he has been in business since 1978. To stay in business that long, he probably does good work and offers good value.
- My dentist proudly displays all her qualifications on the surgery wall: it is safe to use her.
- If your business card or letterhead carries the logo of IBM you will find doors open much more easily than if your business card is for Ace Consulting Emporium, which no one has ever heard of. Clients are not opening their doors to you: they are opening their doors to all that IBM represents.
- If you have a personal introduction to a potential client, you will be more likely to get an appointment than with a cold call.
- Endorsements on your website from current clients reassure new clients.

In most of the cases above, you are implicitly using the endorsement of other clients to attract new clients. If my plumber advertised 'quality, speed and service' it would mean nothing. Anyone can claim that. Not every plumber can claim to have been helping clients since 1978. The exception is the dentist's example: she relies on professional qualifications and affiliations. Many firms do the same by advertising that they belong to various trade bodies. These references are not as powerful as client references: trade bodies often put members, not customers, first.

Risk

Some 74 per cent of the population say that they trust the average person on the street, but only 23 per cent trust politicians. That is probably because most of us have not had the opportunity to be let down by strangers in the street, but we have had plenty of opportunity to be let down by politicians. If we ask directions from a stranger, there is little risk to us. If we are about to commit our firm to a new IT system, there is huge risk for us. Risk grows with the size of the purchase.

> buyers do not want to
> make a mistake

The bigger the decision, the more risk-averse buyers become. For the really big decisions, you need to show huge credibility and you need to show that you are fully on their side (values alignment). Buyers do not want to make a mistake. So their default position is 'do nothing – or as little as possible'.

The obvious way of dealing with risk is to reduce it. But often the best way of dealing with risk is to increase it. Increase risk? Increase the perceived risk of *doing nothing*. This needs to be handled sensitively. Any buyer who feels directly threatened may well lash out. Outline the situation, and let them draw their conclusions. For instance:

- 'This product will be advertised on TV all next month: we are expecting customers to come looking for it.' Unspoken threat: if your store does not feature the product, your customers will go elsewhere.
- 'The price reduction lasts until the end of the month.' Unspoken threat: you will pay more next month.
- 'Our clients tell us that this machine typically drives 20 per cent better productivity and 15 per cent fewer rejects than current machinery.' Unspoken threat: do you really want to be losing out to your competition?
- 'We have already had ten viewings of this property. People seem to love it.' Unspoken threat: if you do not bid now, and high, you will lose it.

The more obvious and common way of handling risk is to reduce it. This is where it is worth remembering that risk comes with the choice of two flavours: logical risk and emotional risk.

Logical risk

Reducing logical risk is fairly straightforward. You can offer a money-back guarantee. The best guarantees are unconditional ones: the more conditions attached to it, the less attractive it is, the less the buyer believes the guarantee and the more the buyer distrusts your product. An unconditional guarantee is a vote of confidence in your offer. Other ways of reducing logical risk include:

- a cooling-off period – trial periods and packages;
- insurance and warranties;
- phasing your project proposal;
- references from existing clients to assure your client.

Emotional risk

Logical risks are relatively easy to deal with, because buyers are happy to talk about them. Buyers are less happy talking about the more important risk: emotional risk. The question nagging in the back of their minds is: 'Will I look foolish to my colleagues, friends and family if I go ahead with this purchase?' Naturally, this is not a risk that buyers voice to the salesperson. Instead, they will raise other risks and concerns which sound logical but are little more than a cover for their fears. This is where things get tricky. Using reason to deal with emotion is like fighting fire with fuel: entertaining, but dangerous. It is a lesson we know from dealing with toddlers who are having a tantrum. The same lesson applies to our customers.

There are two ways of pre-empting perceived emotional risk. The more powerful way is to enlist the support of other clients. If everyone else is wrong, there is no shame in being wrong with the rest of them. Being wrong alone is a very lonely place indeed. If everyone else hires McKinsey, or Accenture or IBM or another market leader, there is no harm in using them as well. They may not be cheap, or innovative, or fast or even good. But at least you did not mess up by hiring some funky boutique that was long on hype and hope and short on results. Of course, not all of us work for market leaders. So that is where we need to use client references – tell the 'what we find' stories about how other clients have worked with us. Client testimonials are far more powerful than anything we claim ourselves. The power of Amazon and some of the leading travel sites lies at least in part in the client reviews of books, restaurants and hotels: they have an emotional credibility that is hard to trump.

The other way of dealing with emotional risk is to give the client a story that shows that they are smart. Give them bragging rights. Give them a story to tell their friends and colleagues about what a smart deal they drove. The story is normally very short and simple:

- I got an extra three years' warranty on my computer.
- I got a stunning trade-in on my old car – above book price.
- I secured the best team for the consulting project we are buying.
- I got them to commit to a special co-promotion on this line of products we are buying.
- This new machine will cut our cycle time by 35 per cent.

None of the examples above needs to cost significant money or erode margin. But all of them give the buyer a story that shows they have been smart. They might have been able to negotiate a better deal overall, but that will be invisible to anyone else. All that matters is that they look good to themselves and to the people who count in their lives. When selling the story to the client, make sure that you give them the script. Do not simply make the concession. Make a song and dance about the concession: 'We don't normally do this but ... I will have to get permission to give you this price/warranty ... getting you the team you want is really hard but ...' If they start to smile and puff their chests up with pride at winning their point, you can inwardly smile and know that you have also just won.

First impressions

Which one of the following two people would you trust most?

A Person in torn jeans, with matted hair, three-day stubble, who rarely turns up before 11 am.

B Person in smart suit, clean-shaven, with polished shoes and smile, firm handshake, well-organised papers.

The chances are that most customers will back B, not A. In doing so they may have chosen to back a corrupt politician, a greedy and incompetent banker or a downright fraudster. Meanwhile, they may have ignored the passionate charity worker, or the brilliant IT specialist or entrepreneur who works all night, is honest and achieves great things.

And that makes the point. First impressions may be completely false, but we are still swayed by them. And that is why all the greatest fraudsters hide behind the sharp suit and smart image: to con people successfully, they have to look like they can be trusted. So they put on the appearances of trust in how they dress, speak and behave.

We should not be judged by how we look, but we are. If we slouch around like a teenager in full hormonal angst waiting for the world to recognise our innate humanity and brilliance, we will have a very long wait.

For better or for worse, there is plenty of evidence that suggests we make our minds up about other people within seconds of meeting them: we either like them or we do not. We have to make those first few seconds work in our favour. There are three things we can do to help ourselves:

● Set the standard before arriving.
● Look the part.
● Act the part.

Set the standard before arriving

First impressions do not start when you first meet someone. They start much earlier. What would you expect of the following three people?

- Anne sent you a company brochure and introductory letter before the meeting. She works for a top investment bank; she is a young vice-president; she graduated top of the class from Cambridge; the letter was on thick paper, with a deeply embossed company logo on top; the letter included a hand-written note in blue ink.
- Bill sent you his company brochure for plumbing supplies. The brochure is full of pictures of smiling plumbers at work; the letter he sent is simple and short and on standard note paper.
- Chris is a final-year undergraduate applying for a job and has sent you a letter. The word-processed document has a few errors in it; the layout is messy; he has spelt your name wrongly.

You will expect Anne, Bill and Chris to be very different sorts of people. You may or may not look forward to meeting each of them. Anne's approach can be as bad as that of Chris: it can look arrogant and smug. Pitch your approach to the person you are meeting.

Your first impressions are not just your introductory email or letter. They are your entire corporate identity: website, Google presence, Facebook, letterhead, logo, brochures, stationery. Be consistent and, if possible, over-invest. Risk-averse buyers want to deal with a low-risk supplier: that means an established, reliable and reputable supplier with a good track record. When you first meet in person, you want the buyer to feel confident that they are meeting the right sort of person.

Look the part

Thirty years ago, a revolution was started by a pair of socks. All the top executives of Procter & Gamble (P&G) marched on stage for a conference. When they sat down, there was a shocked silence:

it was clear that one of the executives was not wearing regulation black socks. He was wearing grey socks. There was a feeling that this was not just subversive: it was downright unpatriotic.

Thirty years later I was speaking at a conference for Skype. The only person not in jeans and T-shirt was the speaker. Even the CEO was in jeans and T-shirt.

The conformity of the past has been replaced by a dazzling diversity of choice. What was simple has become complicated. You have to look like you can be trusted. This leads us to two dress principles:

- Mirror the dress code of the client.
- If in doubt, err on the side of being conservative.

If you insist on a suit and tie when calling on a creative, high-tech outfit where no one even owns a tie, you will look like a stuffed shirt: you will look like a boring, old-fashioned person who does not 'get' their needs or their industry. Equally, turn up casual at the head office of a traditional retail bank, and you will look like you do not care; that you are sloppy and unreliable.

Ideally, the client should not even notice what you are wearing. It should look natural: you should blend in with them. The client should be interested in what you have to offer, not in what you wear.

These things are easier to say than to do. I speak from experience. I turned up to my first job interview (for P&G) in paint-spattered overalls. Despite this, they hired me ... on condition that I buy a suit. When I joined a fancy professional services firm some years later, the partner kindly told me that he would advance me one month's salary ... to buy a decent suit. When I finally became a partner, the senior partner arranged a lunch for me ... with his personal tailor so that I could buy a really good suit. Great dress sense does not come naturally to all of us. Over the years, I have learned that it makes life far easier to dress the part than to do your own, wild and non-conformist thing. Keep your punk hairstyle and clothes strictly for the weekend.

Act the part

How you behave in the first few seconds of a meeting forms impressions very fast. Unfortunately, the first few seconds are when we are likely to be most nervous. Over the years, I have developed a routine to get me over the first few seconds of a meeting. I have

it rehearsed and scripted in my head, so that no matter how nervous I may feel, I can rely on my script, which I adapt for each meeting, conference or speech. We all develop our own scripts:

> hope is not a method and luck is not a strategy

you do not have to copy someone else. Do what works for you. The important thing is to have a plan and have a script. Do not leave it to chance, do not hope to get lucky because hope is not a method and luck is not a strategy.

Here is my routine, when I am waiting in the reception area to be met, or when I am waiting to go on stage for a speech.

- **Remain standing**. Keep the energy levels up and be ready to meet your client on their own level. Avoid the energy rush that comes from suddenly standing up, so that instead you can remain calm and focused.

- **Keep your hands free**. And have all your papers in your bag, ready to be pulled out. If you have got your papers out and need to repack them in front of your client, you look disorganised and fail to engage them: you have missed your chance to make a good impression.

- **Keep the mobile phone turned off**. Fumbling through your pockets to turn off your mobile is not a great way to impress your client.

- **Keep your right hand dry**. Do you really like shaking hands with someone who is nervous and has a sweaty palm?

- **Look for conversation cues**. There will be plenty of cues to pick up, which will allow you to make small talk on the way to the office. Perhaps they are announcing a new product, or the company brochure has a picture of your client, or they are boasting about their community involvement. These cues are a good opportunity to get the client talking about their favourite subject: themselves.

- **Relax**. I breathe deep, relax my shoulders and quietly rehearse what I want to say. I then visualise what a great meeting it is going to be: I can see, hear and feel in detail why I am going to enjoy it. By the time the client arrives, I do not have a frown on my face. I have a relaxed smile ready as my greeting, because that is how I feel.

This preparation is geared to making sure I can engage from the very first second the client walks through the door. I want to focus on them 100 per cent: I do not want to worry about organising my papers, standing up, dealing with my mobile, worrying about a sweaty palm.

None of this preparation works if you turn up late or in a rush. Go to the location early, find the right entrance and then wait in your car until five minutes before the meeting is due. You can always use any spare time to gather some intelligence (check if the place is busy and growing, look to see who else is in the visitors' book, talk to the receptionist, do some last minute preparation). Allow yourself enough time to get through the formalities of reception and security. I used to think of this as nuisance time, lost time; but it is nuisance time only if you choose to waste it. Use it well and it is perfect preparation time.

Partner not vendor

The best salespeople often do not act or sound like salespeople. They act like a partner of their client. Selling is a different way of thinking from partnering, as shown overleaf:

Vendor mindset	Partner mindset
I win, you lose	Win–win for each of us
Sell my idea	Find a solution for you
Focus on my product	Focus on your needs
Sell my perspective	Respect your perspective
Make a sale	Build a relationship
Pitch and talk	Ask questions and listen

The partnership principle is at the heart of great sales, from post room to board room. As buyers, we know this is true: we want to buy from someone we trust, not from someone we do not trust. The vendor mindset sets up a contest. The partner mindset sets up collaboration. The buyer and seller work together to find the best solution.

To become the respected partner of a client, there are at least five things you can do to become your client's trusted partner.

1   **Listen, not talk**. As a partner, you have to see the world through the eyes of the customer. They may be warped eyes, but that does not matter. Perceptions may be false, but the consequences of those perceptions are real. You do not have to agree with the client: you have to understand them. From understanding you may discover more, not fewer, sales possibilities.

2   **Be selfless**. Show that you can be trusted. Give them best advice. Once, I had to hire some lawyers for a sticky case. I approached several firms. All were impressive and they had even more impressive fee structures. They would be happy to help me and to fleece me. Then one firm looked at my case and warned me about the costs: they could spiral out of control. They told me that I should think about asking for a fixed-price fee, and see if the lawyers would be prepared to work at least in

part on the basis of a success fee. If they really think I can win, they should shoulder some of the risk and reward. They were the only firm that was helping me, not helping themselves. It was an easy, and eventually successful, decision.

3   **Be realistic: set expectations well from the start**. It is very easy to over-promise in the desire to seal the deal. That way disaster lies. I started work with Mitsubishi in Japan at the same time as another firm also began a contract with them. Our work was limited and went well. The other firm had promised great things just to get in the door: two years later they were still working, for free, to deliver the promises they made for their first three-month contract. Mitsubishi also sounded bitter about some work by another consulting company. They were so bitter, they had banned this very prestigious firm from working for any part of the group. I later found out the ban had been put in place 25 years earlier and had never been lifted. Setting expectations right can be tough, and may even lose some initial business. But it is the only way to build respect. Expectations can drive a partnership or a divorce for decades.

4   **Don't worry about your sale**. Worry about the relationship. If you can build up a relationship of trust and respect, the business will follow. You do not have to spend months taking clients out to dinner to build trust. You can do it in a few minutes while selling on the shop floor: show interest in the client, interest in what they need. Clients are very good at selling to themselves once they trust you: let them do the hard work for you.

5   **Relax and smile**. My gran told me that 'You're always well dressed if you wear a smile'. She clearly had not been to some of the more depraved undergraduate events where the only thing that anyone was wearing was spaced-out smiles. But the general principle holds true. If you want your partner to relax, you need to relax. Buying is a tense and risky process for many people. Remove the tension, show that you are on their side.

Love your client

This is where I may disappoint you: this is not the guide to sex and selling, although that can work as well. It looks at another question: who is your best prospect for new sales? Answer: your existing clients.

In most industries there is a simple rule of thumb: it costs seven times as much to acquire a new client as it does to sell to an existing client. Not only is it cheaper to sell to existing clients; they also tend to buy a wider range of services, they spend more and they are far more profitable.

There are plenty of reasons why existing clients are better prospects than new clients:

- Existing clients know you and, hopefully, trust you.
- You will know who makes decisions and you will have a good relationship with them.
- You can see which opportunities are emerging in existing clients: you can seal the deal before it ever goes public.

'Love your client' does not fit with the traditional view of selling. Salespeople are often seen as hunters who go out and hunt down the big beast for the big feast. When the beast has been eaten, we then go out and hunt another beast. This traditional and romantic view of selling is true for only a minority of us. For most of us, success does not come from hunting new prospects, but from cultivating and growing existing clients.

> in the new world, we have to be farmers, not hunters

In the new world, we have to be farmers, not hunters. Once you acquire a client, keep the client and grow the relationship. This means that the job is only starting when you make the first sale. The first sale is not a licence to kill the client and feast on the client's bones: it is a licence to nurture the client and milk the client for years to come.

The way this works depends on the business. The simplest sales advice I give to sole traders, like plumbers, electricians and decorators, is to send Christmas cards. It works. We have all had tradesmen come and do repairs, paint or help out. When we find one we can trust, they are like gold dust. But human nature being what it is, it may be three years before we need them again, and by then we have lost their contact details. The Christmas card is an easy way of reminding clients that you are still alive and of giving them your contact details.

Car dealerships normally have details of their clients: they have opportunities not just to send Christmas cards, but also birthday cards and invitations to new product launches. In the same way, the most valuable item an art dealer has is not a painting, it is their client list, which they cultivate assiduously with drinks at regular intervals for new shows. Finding a new art buyer is very hard; getting existing clients to buy again is relatively easy.

Raising the bar

Workers in cubicle land find it hard to show how well they have done. They can point to the number of emails sent, meetings attended and cups of tea they have drunk. All these may be worthwhile activities, but it is hard to point to any positive results at the end of the emailing, meetings and tea drinking.

Fortunately sales performance is much clearer. We either sell or we do not: the number of cups of tea we drink may help us, but it does not count. Even better, there is a very simple formula that shows where we should focus our efforts to raise our performance – see Figure 3.1 overleaf.

Figure 3.1 Simplified sales model

Figure 3.1 shows that there are only three things you can change to improve your sales:

- Approach more targets each day, week or year.
- Improve the conversion rate from targets to sales.
- Increase the value of the average sale.

Most sales training works on the assumption that the only way to increase sales is by improving the conversion rate. This is clearly not true. The other two levers may be at least, if not more, powerful ways of improving sales, as we shall see in the two examples below. As we can see above, the formula works in every environment: it works as well for a trainee salesperson working in an electrical goods store as well as it works for the sophisticated partner in a consulting firm. They both must sell to survive and they are both subject to the same success formula.

Let's look at how the typical consulting partner can raise her game. She is an average consulting partner, pulling in about £4.5 million of revenues a year, against an annual target of £4 million to £5 million. She wants to do better than average. So she looks at the statistics for the best-selling partner in her group, and Figure 3.2 shows what she finds.

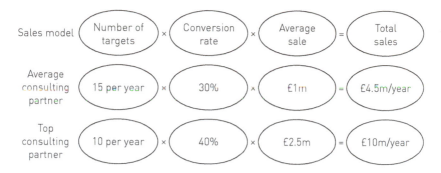

Figure 3.2 Raising the bar: professional services

The message is pretty clear. She has been chasing the low-hanging fruit and going after too many potential leads. The best-selling partner chases fewer leads that are better qualified and have higher potential value. And he plays to win: so his conversion rate is slightly higher (40 per cent versus 30 per cent) but the big difference is that he sells big: his average project size is £2.5 million versus £1 million. They land up with roughly the same number of clients each year (4 versus 4.5), but the best partner builds deep relationships and big projects. Looking more closely, it was clear that the higher project value and higher conversion rate did not come from new clients: it came from building relationships with existing clients. The average partner was doing well at gaining new clients, but first projects tend to be smaller and less profitable for the firm. She saw the way to double sales is by selling less, but selling smarter. She started to focus more on building existing clients rather than hunting for new ones.

A similar story can be told for the trainee salesperson selling in store. The trainee looked at what the average and the best salespeople achieved. Figure 3.3 shows what he found.

Figure 3.3 Raising the bar: in-store sales

As shown by Figure 3.3:

● The best salespeople work harder: they approach more potential clients than the average salesperson. Persistence pays.

● The best salespeople sell up: they sell premium models and are better at selling the extras such as insurance, delivery and installation.

● The best salespeople have a slightly lower conversion rate than average, which is not surprising: they are approaching more people and trying to sell them more. But they are not afraid of rejection.

The success formula is different in every business. Work out the success formula in your business and decide where you want to focus. You have a choice:

● **Work harder**: approach more clients.

● **Improve your conversion rate**: build your sales skills.

● **Sell up**: increase the average value of every sale.

Clearly, understanding the success formula is only the first step. The second step is to learn what your most successful salespeople do and how they do it. Fortunately, most salespeople are proud of what they do and are more than happy to share their knowledge: all you have to do is ask.

Learning to succeed

Successful people are always learning and improving. Just like top sports stars or musicians, they never stop training. And they are not just practising the fancy skills: they keep on working at the basic skills. Fancy skills are useless if you cannot get the basics right. The sales challenge is how to learn when so much of our selling is done alone: there is no one to coach us, observe us or help us.

HE LEARNS FROM HIS MISTAKES: IN FACT, THE TERM 'LIFETIME LEARNING' MIGHT HAVE BEEN COINED FOR HIM

ROGER BEALE

One answer is to go on sales training courses. They can help. But there is an even better source of help. The best sales trainer might have 20 or 30 years of experience, most of which will be outside your sales category. But in your sales organisation you might have 100 people, each with 15 years of experience. Collectively, you have 50 times as much experience of a top sales trainer, and all that experience is directly relevant to your success. If you are surrounded by 1,500 years of relevant experience, use it.

Organise your weekly or monthly sales meetings so that there is an experience-sharing slot. This is the chance both to learn from others and to show off your own knowledge.

Break your sales process down into bite-sized chunks: identifying prospects, getting the first meeting, preparation, building rapport, qualifying the client, qualifying on price, qualifying the issue, gaining agreement to the issue, sizing the opportunity, suggesting the idea, overcoming objections (there can be many of these), closing and following up. There is plenty here for many training sessions:

- Choose one bite-sized chunk for each training session. Focus on a little and do it well: make it as concrete and as practical as possible.

- Brainstorm all the ideas the team has on how to tackle the issue. Go for quantity, not quality. Avoid any criticism, which may make you look smart but will encourage everyone else to shut up. List the ideas on a flip chart so that everyone can see that their idea has been heard and recognised.

- Vote on the best ideas. Give everyone three votes and use Chicago rules. Chicago rules are that there are no rules. Anyone cheating gets to do sentry duty with the fishes at the bottom of the local river. This avoids all the discussion about 'Can I use all my votes for one topic?' or 'Can I merge ideas?' Ugh.

- Discuss the best ideas. Is there anything to stop us using this? How will we do this in practice?

- Now write up the ideas in a best-practice handbook, which everyone receives. The ideas work because:

  - They come from the team, not the boss.

  - They are practical: they do not come from a trainer or textbook.

  - They are relevant and credible: they have already worked for team members.

- Repeat the exercise at your next sales meeting for the next topic. Slowly, you will build up a handbook of sales best practice.

- After about 18 months, start the whole process again: refresh people's memory and help newcomers. You will find that people learn far more from the discussion than they do from the handbook. The process is even more important than the output.

Never, never stop learning.

Positive outlook

A positive outlook is not just at the heart of successful selling. It is at the heart of a successful life. Fortunately, it is an outlook that can be acquired, and it is well worth acquiring. In this section we will explore:

- Why a positive outlook is important in sales and in life.
- What a positive outlook is … and is not.
- How you can build a positive outlook.

Why a positive outlook is important in sales and in life

I had the fortune to be on the board of the Well-being Institute at Cambridge University. They do wonderful and rigorous research into how people live and age well. They quickly found that people who led happy, fulfilled lives lived longer and better than most other people. 'Be happy or die' seemed to be the simple conclusion. As one of the world's natural worriers, this gave me something more to worry about: the more I worried, the more likely I was to die, which gave me even more to worry about.

The landmark piece of research which they often quoted involved nuns. Nuns are a very useful study group: they all live essentially the same life style with the same diet. There are not many variables to control for. The researchers looked at the statements the young nuns had made when they first entered their nunnery decades ago.

Many of the nuns talked about duty, commitment to Christ and other predictable reasons for entering the nunnery. A few nuns were different. They talked with enthusiasm about how lucky they were to have this chance to fulfil their dreams: it was everything they had ever hoped for. The 'duty' nuns all died before the 'lucky' nuns. Attitudes and beliefs really can kill you or save you.

So what has this got to do with selling? Everything.

If you are not enthusiastic, energetic and positive about yourself, no one else will be for you. If you do not believe in your product, no one else will. Enthusiasm and pessimism are infectious. I once heard a talk by Patrick Moore, the famous and eccentric British astronomer. I hate astronomy: it is very

> if you do not believe in your product, no one else will

technical and I can never see any stars anyway through the light pollution of the city. But Patrick Moore is one of the world's great enthusiasts. He makes distant blobs in the sky, which I can't see, seem wildly exciting. By the end of his talk I found myself feverishly exploring options for buying telescopes, even though I knew a telescope would be more or less useless for me: city lights, heat pollution and cloud cover mean that even the moon rarely shows its face. He had sold me on astronomy through sheer self-belief and wild enthusiasm for his subject.

Large swathes of business treat enthusiasm as a certifiable mental disorder. As a result, many managers live in dull, monochrome organisations where the most exciting thing they do is to analyse variance on the monthly budget reports. This is wonderful news. It makes it far easier for you to stand out. Where others find problems, you should find solutions; where others soak up energy, you should create energy; where others see a glass half empty, you should see a glass half full.

What a positive outlook is ... and is not

Being positive has to be real. It is not about putting on a synthetic smile and saying 'Have a nice day' through gritted teeth. False enthusiasm is as authentic as a seven pound note: people see through it very fast. You have to cultivate a genuinely positive outlook. Here are the top ten behaviours to grow:

1 Believe in what you sell, not just in selling for the sake of it.
2 Enjoy what you do, not just as a means to earn a salary.
3 See opportunities, not just problems.
4 Focus on outcomes, not on obstacles.
5 See every challenge as an opportunity to learn, grow and develop, not as a setback.
6 Be curious about your business: always seek to learn more.
7 Have wide interests beyond selling: show enthusiasm in all parts of life.
8 Go above and beyond to help your colleagues, clients and friends.
9 Complement and support, rather than criticise (not even competitors).
10 Find the positives in every situation.

These characteristics are the same whether you are on the shop floor selling light bulbs, or you are a partner in the board room selling professional services. I have worked with positive and negative examples of both light bulb salespeople and partners: the positive versions outsell, outperform and outlast the negative versions by a very large margin.

How you can build a positive outlook

In the film *Flash Gordon*, the evil emperor Ming ordered all creatures of the universe to rejoice, on pain of death. Forcing people to rejoice, be happy, cheer up or be positive is like trying to squeeze the toothpaste back into the toothpaste tube. It does not work.

There are some simple tricks we can use to make ourselves feel and act positively or negatively. The most important, and simplest, is to count our blessings.

Professor Richard Wiseman has studied lucky people. He finds several things about them. First, they simply try harder. One lady keeps on winning free goods, free holidays, free cars and even free money. It is astounding luck. Except that she enters over 200 competitions every week. And the more she enters competitions, the more skill she acquires in winning them. So her luck is not luck: it is practice and persistence. Lucky salespeople display the same persistence and commitment.

Wiseman also found that lucky people simply think of themselves as lucky, and unlucky people think they are unlucky. As a simple exercise, think about what happened to you today:

- How many lights were at red on the way in to work?
- How many other drivers cut you up, delayed you or did unexpected things?
- How many bad news stories did you hear on the news?
- What went wrong at work today: delays, setbacks, time-wasting requests, junk emails, pointless meetings?
- How are you doing with the tax return, utility bills, repairs, washing and maintenance at home?

Think about your day this way, and every day becomes a struggle against insurmountable odds. Lucky and positive people see the world differently and ask different questions:

- How many green lights did I pass on the way to work today?
- What went well today: small progress on a big project, sales made or started, crises dealt with or averted, routine work accomplished?
- How many 'thank yous' did I give or receive? Who did I help and who helped me?

- What did I enjoy most: some music, a radio show, some great scenery on the way to work, my family and friends, a good meal?
- What did I learn from some of the more interesting challenges today?
- How will I make tomorrow even better?

Ask these questions, and the abysmal day that comes out of the first, negative, set of questions transforms itself into a great day. The same day has a completely different complexion depending on how we choose to see it. Ultimately, we are responsible for our own feelings. If we want to feel gloomy and negative, that is our choice and we will find plenty of reasons to justify our choice. If we want to feel positive and good, we can find plenty of reasons to do so. It pays to look at the world from the right perspective.

Even little things, like our routine for getting up in the morning can have a huge effect on our whole day, as I discovered:

How to get up in the morning

One day I woke up in a mud hut in the middle of Africa, where I was doing some research on tribal societies. The nearest water was a five-kilometre walk away in a muddy river infested with crocodiles. All the water was carried by women, in pots on their heads. Heating the water required gathering firewood and making a fire.

At the end of the research trip I got back to a small town on the edge of civilisation. I checked into the finest hotel in town, which had corrugated iron for a roof and barbed wire for a fence. But it had a real bed and a bathroom of sorts. I woke up in the morning and went to the bathroom, and a miracle happened. I turned a tap and cold, clean, running water came out. I then turned another tap and another miracle happened: hot water came flowing out. No need to walk five kilometres through the bush; no need to gather firewood. When you start the day with two miracles in two minutes, the rest of the day has to be brilliant.

▶

And now, even in London, I wake up in the morning and discover the miracles of hot and cold water. And then everything else is like a miracle as well: electricity, transport, comfortable chairs, telephones. These are all things we take for granted. We do not appreciate them because they are so commonplace. But if we really learn to count our blessings and value what we have, then every day becomes a day of wonder and a day of joy. It becomes impossible to have anything other than a positive outlook.

In contrast, if your day starts by listening to the news as the radio wakes you up, it becomes pretty hard to feel positive about anything. Before you get out of bed, you will find yourself in the company of lying politicians, incompetent officials, greedy business people, wars, disasters and disease. The world will look a pretty bleak sort of place, and there will be nothing you can do about any of the disasters that are served up to you on the radio. You will be powerless in the face of a dismal world.

High aspirations: focus on outcomes

Low aspirations are always self-fulfilling. If you believe something is impossible, it will not be possible for you. If you think you cannot sell a product or sell to a certain client, you will successfully not sell. As with selling, so with life. I started a charity working with the toughest schools: they are deserts of low aspirations. No one believes in the kids and so the kids do not believe in themselves. They get lousy grades and are more likely to graduate to prison than to university. But give them a chance and they change: once they believe they can win, they do.

Dare to believe. When President Kennedy announced that America would send 'a man to the moon and bring him back again within ten years' it was a statement of the impossible. Except that he did not see it that way. 'We do these things' he said 'not because they are easy, but because they are difficult, they are the test of our character and determination.' In 1969 Armstrong took his 'One small step for man, one giant leap for mankind' and the impossible had become reality. Along the way, there had been huge problems and setbacks. Losing a Gemini mission and its astronauts on the launch pad would have ruined or delayed most projects. It simply became another challenge to overcome on the path to success, which is rarely smooth or easy.

All the great empires have been built by people who did not understand the word 'impossible'. The Brits did not understand that they lived on a small wet island on the edge of the North Atlantic: they built the largest empire in history, ushered in the industrial revolution and changed the world for ever. Alexander the Great should have realised that he

> we are only as great as we dare to be

ruled a tin-pot state on the edge of Greek civilisation. By the age of 25 he had conquered the entire civilised world and overthrown the ancient empire of Persia. We all remember Alexander the Great; who remembers his uncle Alexander the Reasonable? We are only as great as we dare to be.

Inevitably, there is a huge gap between aspirations and reality. Hoping to succeed is different from succeeding. We need to turn daydreams into reality. To turn aspirations into success, you need a spine of steel, not a wobbling jelly of hope. At the heart of the spine of steel is a relentless focus on outcomes.

There is an old Irish joke about a traveller in the far west of Ireland. He asks a local how to get to Dublin. The local scratches his head and then pronounces: 'If I was going to Dublin, I wouldn't start from here.' That is the problem. If we focus on where we are now, we will probably realise that our destination is too far away. So we give up. Gurus often advise 'first things first'. That is catastrophic advice for anyone with an ounce of ambition. Start at the end. Decide where you want to get to, and then work back from there. Divide your journey, your goal, into bite-sized chunks. Work out where you want to be in five years' time: so where does that mean you need to be by the end of this year, this month, this week and today? So what do you do now? If you follow the 'first things first' advice, you will follow a random walk from the past to the future. You will do what is most important for today, which may not be what is most important for tomorrow. Today, the most important thing might be filing your expenses claim on time to stop the accounts department whining at you. For the future, the most important thing might be going on a sales course, spending time with a great salesperson, or starting a discussion with a big but long-term prospect. Focusing on outcomes means starting with the end in mind.

Focusing on outcomes works on any time horizon you want.

- **Over your lifetime**. As a simple but morbid exercise, write your own obituary. What do you want it to say? What do you think it will say? What are you going to do to close the gap? Turn the exercise around: how do you remember 2005, or 2000 or 1995? There are some years where I have no memories. All I achieved was to get one year closer to death. Those are not good years. How will you make this year memorable, in work and beyond? Live life with the record button on, not the erase button on.

- **Over your career**. Where do you want to get to? What are the skills and experiences you need to build to get there? What does that imply you need to be doing over the next three to five years? I interviewed two people for a sales job. At the end, I let them ask any questions they wanted. The first person asked if I would raise her starting salary 10 per cent to make it competitive with another offer. The second person asked me what it would take for her to earn ten times her starting salary within ten years. I hired the second person: she had real ambition and was thinking long term. She now earns nearly 20 times what I first paid her. Do you want to maximise your short-term or long-term potential?

- **Over five years.**What sort of role do you want to be in within five years: selling, key account management, sales director? What will it take for you to get there? Again, the high-paying job today may be less attractive than a job that starts with a lower salary but has much higher prospects.

- **This year**. Are you in the right role to achieve your five-year and career ambitions? What sort of sales funnel do you need to achieve your sales goal? Are you chasing short-term opportunities at the expense of ignoring bigger opportunities which need more time and investment? Or are you betting everything on the one big prize in the fourth quarter and ignoring the low-hanging fruit which is available today? Start at the end and work back from there.

- **In this conversation**. How many times have you been dragged into a pointless argument with buyers, bosses or colleagues? Rarely does anyone come out of such conversations looking good. Even if you win an argument, you lose a friend. That is an expensive loss for a minor gain. Look ahead to where you want to be at the end of the conversation: start with the outcome. The best outcome may be to let the other person calm down and find another time when you can have a more reasoned discussion. Starting at the end gets to a better outcome than being carried away by the emotion of the moment.

Starting at the end liberates us from the tyranny of the past. The past is over. There is nothing we can do about it. But we can change the future. Starting at the end gives clarity and focus about what we need to do now. And it should give us a sense of urgency about starting now.

The Duke of Wellington displayed this urgency when he met one of his gardeners having a break. 'What are you doing?' asked the Iron Duke. 'Planting an avenue of oak trees. Neither you nor I will see them in all their glory: that will be a hundred years from now' replied the gardener. 'What!' exclaimed Wellington. 'In that case there is not a moment to lose!' and he picked up a shovel and started digging a hole for the oak tree.

If you need to do it, do it now.

Escape the comfort zone

The most lethal form of failure is success – when you find your comfort zone. We have all seen colleagues like this. They have their sales territory and they have their tame customers. They know exactly what they have to do to meet sales targets each year. If there is an attractive sales contest which they want to win, they can do deals with their friendly customers, stuff the sales channels and win the sales sprint. They then give their customers a holiday: the customers do not need to buy any more while they unwind the excess stock which they purchased.

The comfort zone is the death zone for ambition. Living in the comfort zone is to retire in post. The quiet life looks attractive. But in the next recession or restructuring, only the hungry will survive. Life in the comfort zone may be quiet, but it is dangerous. To survive, you have to be improving all the time.

Improving is more than going on training courses. We have to try to test things ourselves. Inevitably, we make mistakes. It is only when we make mistakes, only when we fail, that we know we are pushing ourselves and learning. If we never make a mistake, we never learn. Fear of failure is the greatest barrier to self-improvement.

> if we never make a mistake, we never learn

I discovered the importance of making mistakes when I first went skiing. We started out on the nursery slopes with an instructor telling us to 'Bend zee knees!' as we cautiously did some snowplough turns. There was one idiot who tried doing the fancy turns. He was the class joker. He was always falling down as he tried the fancy turns. How we laughed as we slowly went past him while he spat snow out of his mouth. By the end of the week we stopped laughing. We were still on the nursery slopes doing snowplough turns and bending zee knees. He was flying down intermediate and even black slopes because he had mastered the fancy turns required for the fancy slopes. He was having a great holiday and we were left cursing him and ourselves. He had set himself a high aspiration ('black slopes by the end of the week') and had pushed himself, and was not afraid to fail. We had started with first things first: bending zee knees and snowplough turns. He achieved, we failed.

Take control

The best book you never need buy is called *Control Your Destiny or Someone Else Will*. It was written about the legendary CEO of General Electric, Jack Welch. The reason it is a great book and you don't need to buy it, is because the title says it all. Many managers drift around in the bowels of their organisations: they shuffle emails, ride successful bandwagons, jump from sinking ships and occasionally fight fires while mixing their metaphors. Drifting is a luxury that you cannot afford. Results are painfully obvious: we succeed, or we do not.

Take control of your world, rather than letting the world control you.

I hear a familiar refrain from salespeople who are struggling. They complain about their boss, their company, their products, their pricing and the support they receive. They present themselves as victims of their world. I have been a victim many times, but only of my own stupidity. If you work for a lousy boss in a lousy company with lousy products, lousy pricing and lousy service, whose fault is that? And what are you going to do about it?

We always have choices. They may not always be comfortable choices. To live in the corporate world is to experience getting let down, done over and cheated. It happens. In one three-year period I managed to be cheated to the tune of $500,000, then $5 million and finally somewhere around $50 million. At least that was progress: the disasters were getting larger and larger each time. And whose fault was it that I was cheated? Mine. By the end of that three-year period I had some awkward choices to make: do I carry on (and be cheated again) or do I change, with all the risks and uncertainties that implied? We naturally cling on to what we have long after it is sane to do so. It takes courage to start over and begin a new adventure, but that is the choice we have to make if we want to control our destiny.

The single most important choice we have is the choice of who we work for. In this respect you are lucky to work in sales. The chances are that you have skills that you can transfer from one employer to another, and you have a clear track record which anyone can understand. Our managerial colleagues are less lucky. If you have spent the last ten years doing settlements in the tripartite asset collateralised repo market you may be well paid, but the chances are that there are not many other employers who need your esoteric skill set.

Instead of making excuses, make decisions: do not whine about the employer, find an employer you want to work for. As you think about your choices, there are some good reasons for moving and for not moving.

Reasons for moving include:

- I do not enjoy what I am doing. The acid test is how I feel when I get up and go to work: am I looking forward to it, or dreading it?
- I am not gaining the skills and experience that I need to enhance my career.

Poor reasons for moving might be:

- I do not like my boss. This is the most common reason people move, but it is dangerous. In practice, the corporate carousel keeps moving and you and your boss are likely to part ways within a year or 18 months. And your boss in a new organisation is going to be a lucky dip: they may or may not be better and they may or may not last long.

- I want an increase in salary. One of my biggest career mistakes was to move for a five-fold increase in salary. The money was great and the employer and the job were useless. The only value of the job was to anchor salary discussions with my next employer at a vastly inflated rate.

- I think the grass is greener elsewhere. A prospective employer always presents their best face to you: the reality may be very different once you are inside. Remember that the grass is greenest where it rains the most.

Listen to your heart (do I enjoy what I do?) and to your head (am I gaining the right skills and experience?). If you enjoy what you do and are getting the right experience, then everything else, including income, will fall into place. Take control of your destiny.

Chapter 4

The sins of selling: how to fail

n practice, we learn as much (if not more) from our failures than we do from our successes. We can hear all the obvious stuff, but it is only when we fail that we truly understand how important the obvious stuff is, and how difficult it is to use common sense consistently. As George Orwell wrote: 'To see what is in front of one's nose needs a constant struggle.' Looking back over my many failures, the causes of them have been, roughly:

- Not listening and understanding properly: 40 per cent.
- Not putting in the effort, not enough resilience: 25 per cent.
- Not engaging the client personally, no rapport: 20 per cent.
- Ignoring the PASSION logical flow: 10 per cent.
- Putting my foot in my mouth and shooting it/other creative mess-ups: 5 per cent.
- Failing to master the reverse flip-flop bi-active power close: 0 per cent.

Having worked with many thousands of salespeople, I can identify the most common causes of failure. The good news is that they are all simple, basic mistakes which can easily be avoided. Obvious? Of course. Do they make the difference between failure and success? Always. As you read through them, take comfort:

- If you have messed up in this way, you are not alone.
- If you have not messed up this way, you are doing very well.

We can learn from painful and personal experience. It is quicker and less painful to learn from the mistakes of others. So here are ten of the most common mistakes:

1 Fear of failure.

2 The 'me' trap.

3 The friend trap.

4 Underselling.

5 Overselling.

6 The work trap.

7 The wrong problem.

8 The logic trap.

9 The wrong firm, wrong boss.

10 Excuses.

Fear of failure

John F. Kennedy once said: 'Only those who dare to fail greatly can ever achieve greatly.' To succeed, you must dare to sell greatly. We only know that we have pushed ourselves to the limits when we exceed them and fall over. If we have not failed, we have not tried hard enough.

We can go to any number of sales training courses and be taught how to close, or how to pre-empt objections, or how to plan. And when I am told such things I think they sound reasonable. Sort of. But it is only when I do not follow the advice and see disaster ensue that I really learn why these things are so important.

School teaches us that failure is bad. As humans, we do not want to fail. But if we always hide from failure, we will not learn and we will never achieve our full potential. Fugitives from failure always seek the easy sale, the easy client, the easy opportunity. In the short term, it works. In the long term, it leads nowhere. The path to success is littered with failures. At the time, each failure is painful.

Over the years, each failure becomes a rich source of learning and of the stories and legends which all salespeople relish.

Our failures, as much as our successes, make us and define us.

The 'me' trap

I listened to a strong CEO speak to a packed hall of potential customers and partners. Aidan, the CEO, was passionate about his business. He spoke with elegance, belief and commitment about his firm; he was a role model for energy, commitment and pride. As speeches go, it was a powerful speech.

After he spoke, there was not much time for anyone else to speak. A bare three minutes was all that was left for Iqbal, the CEO of a much smaller and less prestigious company, to speak. He spoke quietly and calmly, outlining what his company did in a few seconds, and then spent the rest of the time talking about how he could help the various organisations in the room. He said he wanted to meet them and he would be at the back of the hall at the end of the event.

I listened and watched what happened. By lunchtime, Iqbal had exchanged business cards with over 50 potential partners and customers. They were all keen to do business. I then heard a few comments about Aidan, who had been so passionate about his business:

- 'Only interested in himself.'
- 'What had he got for us?'
- 'Very arrogant: I'm not going to work with him.'

I talked to Aidan. He was delighted with his performance. He was convinced he had made a brilliant pitch. Being polite, no one told him to his face that he was a disaster. But if he had watched, he would have seen all his potential customers gathering around his rival. His brilliant speech had been losing his company customers every minute he spoke.

Aidan had fallen into the classic 'me' trap. It is human nature to be proud of what we do and to want to tell everyone else about it. Talking about our product is as exciting to clients as sharing our holiday snaps with strangers. It is very exciting to us and a total turn-off to our clients.

Your starting point should not be your product and yourself. You have to start with the client and the client's needs. See the world through their eyes, and you can succeed.

The friend trap

We all like to be liked. As social animals, we want to have friends. The paranoia induced by Facebook, which tells us all precisely how many 'friends' we have, is just a symptom of this need.

Wanting to be liked is a dangerous trap. You do not need to be liked: you need to be respected. Wanting to be liked leads to weakness. You may get the sale, but you are unlikely to achieve the best price or the biggest sale if you want to accommodate your buyer.

you do not need to be liked: you need to be respected

The way you earn respect is by building trust: listen to the client's needs and then find the best solution for them. Occasionally, you may need to walk away from a sale if that is not the best thing for the client. It may also mean having an awkward conversation with the client: showing why they need to spend more or buy differently to achieve their aims.

As a buyer, I have plenty of friends from whom I would not buy a postage stamp, let alone a car. Perhaps I mix with the wrong sorts of people. When it comes to buying anything of substance, I want to deal with someone who is professional, expert and trustworthy. I do not need to be friends with them. If I respect and trust them, I will buy from them.

Friendship is the low road to weakness; respect is the high road to success.

Underselling

The first time I made a sale to a CEO I was very full of myself. I had been working on a project alone and had convinced the CEO to do another month of work with us. I went back to the office and started strutting my stuff and bragging to whoever would listen, which seemed to mean that I was left talking to the water cooler. Eventually, the senior partner pulled me aside and asked the simple question: 'How much?'

I had not actually price-qualified my sale. Whoops. So I blurted out a figure that I hoped the CEO would accept when I saw him the next day. The senior partner shook his head in disbelief. 'Triple the price' he said and walked away. I was left doing a good impersonation of a fish out of water, with my mouth wide open and a look of goggle-eyed disbelief. With some nerves, I went back to the CEO and, as casually as possible, mentioned the (tripled) price. He did not blink an eyelid: it is what he had expected.

Underselling is a classic symptom of lack of confidence. We do not really believe in the value of our product or service and do not charge for it properly. We under-price or over-promise our deliverables. Either way, we commit our employer to unprofitable business. Any fool can sell unprofitable business: your job is to sell profitable business, not unprofitable business.

There are two keys to avoiding the underselling trap:

- Believe in the full value of your product or service.
- Understand the value of your product or service from the buyer's point of view.

You may know that your product already has an 80 per cent profit margin built in. This could lead you to think that you can discount to gain a sale, and still make a profit. That is lost profit: the buyer does not care if you make an 80 per cent profit or an 80 per cent loss on each sale. Your profits are irrelevant. If your offer has value to the client and better value than that of competitors, then the buyer will buy. Sell to value, not to price.

Overselling

When the buyer is ready to buy, stop selling. Close the sale and shut up. The more you say, the more you can undermine the sale.

Overselling is a natural trap, especially if you are enthusiastic. We see a buyer who looks interested and that encourages us: we talk more and more about the wonders of our product and service. This leads to two potential disasters:

- **'I didn't realise ...'** You say something and a look of surprise sweeps across your buyer's face, as they blurt out 'I didn't realise ...'. They have suddenly spotted a flaw with your offering. The easy sale has just flown out of the window.

- **'Thank you very much ...'** The more you extol the virtues of what your firm can do, how you can help and what you can deliver, the more you are committing yourself. The client may well not have expected so much. The smart buyer will keep quiet and let you go on over-promising, while thinking 'Thank you very much ... Christmas has come early this year'.

Read the buying signals. When the buyer is ready to buy, let them buy. Make it easy for them and easy for you.

The work trap

I once spent an entire day observing the sales in a retail store. My main conclusion at the end of the day was that watching people work is far more congenial than doing the work. And selling is hard work. There are plenty of alternatives to the grind of selling:

- going to meetings;
- filling in paperwork and expenses forms;
- fixing the car, arranging travel;
- doing preparation;

- going to a conference;
- having lunch;
- checking emails and the internet.

Clearly, if you work in a staff function, you can make an entire career out of these non-work activities. Unlike staff people, selling is very transparent. If we are not selling, we are not working. While preparation is vital, it is not a substitute for selling. Unlike the pen pushers in cubicle land, you know when you have succeeded. And success is a function of a very simple formula:

$$(\text{Number of calls}) \times (\text{Conversion rate}) \times (\text{Average sale value}) = \text{Total sales value}$$

If you know your sales target, and you can estimate your average sale and predicted conversion rate, then you know how many calls you need to make to achieve your goal. And each day of the month you can see your progress towards that goal.

The discipline of calling patterns and sales targets helps to achieve sales focus. But it is only a small part of the solution. Ultimately, we only sell if we enjoy it. If we have to force ourselves out of bed and out of the office to sell, then we are probably in the wrong job. Enjoy the job for what it is, with all its ups and downs: we should not work because we have to, but because we want to.

The wrong problem

I got my big break: the chance to present to the board of the company. I rehearsed like crazy. I had 200 pages of slides; I was ready for anything they might ask. I made my pitch, which went as well as I could make it go. At the end there was an awkward silence, broken by a quiet cough from the CEO, sitting at the far end of the vast board room table.

'That was a very impressive presentation' he said, as I puffed myself up with pride. 'I only have one question: what, precisely, was the problem you were solving?' I was ready for any question, except that one. I promptly deflated into an agony of despair.

When selling, the wrong problem trap normally shows up in one of two ways:

- The buyer loses interest: fidgeting, looking away, checking their watch. We are simply not engaging with the buyer. We are not dealing with anything that matters to them.
- Objections start flying. This quickly gets ugly: the more you try to knock the objections down, the more the buyer digs in with more objections and questions. It becomes a lose–lose discussion.

Where you have the wrong problem, stop. Do not keep pushing or trying to deal with the objections. Go back and review the buyer's situation. Confirm, refine or change the agreed problem or opportunity that the client faces. Only when you have the right problem can you make the right sale, or any sale.

The logic trap

Most sales training deals with the logic of selling: identify the problem, show the benefits and deal with the objections. This is good. And it is not enough. You have to go much further. You need to engage with the client. You do not have to make friends with the client, but you must build trust and respect. You know you are bringing the client on to your side when they go into 'noddy' mode: the client starts nodding in agreement, even if it is only about some common interest or past event.

Once you build the bond of respect and trust, selling becomes easier:

● You increase the chances of success.

● You can sell more.

● The client will bring you more opportunities.

The logic trap is deadly because its costs are invisible. With logic you can still make sales, with effort. But you never see the opportunities the client does not bring to you; you never know of the chance to sell more and sell at a better price. You still sell, so you think you have succeeded. It is a failure that seems painless, until you see your rivals selling in products and services and you are left thinking 'Why didn't I get that opportunity?'

The logic trap can keep you in a box the buyer calls 'vendor'. If you go beyond logic and build trust and respect, you move into a box the buyer calls 'partner'. Partners get far more sales than remote vendors.

The wrong firm, wrong boss

We all like to moan about our bosses. We are all convinced we could do a better job than they do. When coaching salespeople, I find that bosses are the number-one source of complaints. Sometimes, I will hear complaints about how dreadful both the boss and the company is: they make life difficult and selling harder. So what do you do if you find you have to sell the wrong products at the wrong price at the wrong time, without enough support?

It is very easy to fix all these problems: move to a better company.

If you find yourself falling into victim mentality, it is time to stop selling. Blaming the rest of the world is not the highway to success. If you have an abysmal boss and firm, then whose responsibility is that? Who decided to work there? And who can do anything about it? It is our responsibility to find the context where we can succeed.

> blaming the rest of the world is not the highway to success

Excuses

Setbacks are a natural part of sales. No one can have a 100 per cent success record: anyone who claims to succeed 100 per cent of the time is either lying or not trying hard enough. You only know that you have pushed yourself to the limit when you go too far: failure is a sign of pushing the limits, so we should accept it and learn from it.

So we need a way of distinguishing between occasional setbacks, which even heroes have, and the death spiral of underperformance. Fortunately, it is very easy to spot the difference. Here is how you can look good even in adversity – and how you can adopt a coat of Teflon which stops muck sticking to you:

- Confront the setback; do not hide it.
- Seek help; do not apportion blame.
- Drive to action; do not indulge in analysis.

- Learn from it; do not start the 'I said she said you said they said' discussion.
- Accept responsibility; do not make excuses.

The death spiral reaction is also clear in the list above. It is a quick way to lose the confidence of clients, colleagues and bosses all at the same time. This is what you do:

- Deny the problem really exists.
- Blame the product, the price, the client, the support.
- Be defensive.
- Undercommunicate; do not seek help.

We all make mistakes, but we should not make excuses. We know that success is in our hands. As one of my early managers told me bluntly: 'Take responsibility or take a hike.' Since then, I have realised that I have often been a victim, but only of my own folly. Once we take responsibility, we can take control of our destiny, learn from mistakes and grow in strength.

Part 2

The practice of selling

was waiting outside the board room of a major bank in Tokyo. I was meant to be selling to them, but it seemed far removed from selling nappies to chemists in Birmingham, where I had started. The differences were obvious:

- The sales cycle was months, not minutes.
- The size of sale was 1,000 times greater.
- I was selling to an institution, not to an individual.
- Politics seemed as important as reason.
- The service was customised to the customer's needs, not our standard product.
- They spoke a different language.

But as I finished my preparations, I realised that the principles of selling applied as much in a Tokyo bank as they did in a Birmingham chemist's shop:

1 Listen.
2 Help more than sell.
3 Focus on the client's needs, not on my needs.
4 Be expert, but don't talk down.
5 Give the client time and space.
6 Make it simple for the client: avoid confusion through too much choice.
7 Focus on benefits to the client, not features of the product.
8 Build trust, but never say 'Trust me'.
9 Give the client a story to tell their peers that shows that they bought smart and got a good deal.
10 Be positive and enthusiastic throughout.

I had slowly arrived at what is technically known as a BFO: a blinding flash of the obvious. The principles of selling may be the same everywhere, but the way they are applied varies greatly.

To achieve sales mastery, we have to do more than master the principles of selling. We have to master selling in our particular context: our industry, our products and services and our sales environment. To simplify things, there are four classic sales environments:

- transaction selling: one to one;
- bids and tenders;
- key account management;
- relationship management.

Part 1 of this book focused on the principles of selling, mainly in the one-to-one environment. Part 2 shows how the same principles can be adapted and applied to the other three environments as well. You can read every section, or focus on the one that is most relevant to you. Below is a short guide to help you decide where to focus.

Transaction selling

Much sales training is focused here: it is where the classic principles of selling are most easily observed and learned. Transaction sales typically have the following characteristics:

- The sales are relatively infrequent. How often do you replace your computer, get a plumber, buy a house or buy a car? Probably not often, and maybe not from the same person each time. But, in each case, a good salesperson will help you buy from them, not from someone else.
- The product is relatively simple: there is little by way of true customisation. Any customer choice is fairly limited.
- The sales process is short and simple: often the selling is simply one to one, or maybe one to a family.
- The sale is likely to be a single transaction, rather than a part of a wider relationship. Some people have relationships with their IT supplier, most prefer not to.

Bids and tenders

As with the retail transaction, bids happen fairly rarely. A typical example might be public sector procurement. By definition, they are not meant to be decisions based on relationships. But, unlike the retail sale, bids can be horrendously complicated:

- The sales cycle can take months or even years.
- The buying process is complicated.
- The network of buyers involved can be extensive.
- Negotiation skills are at a premium.
- The sales effort is likely to be a team effort.

Predictably, there is a grey area between retail sales and bid management: buying a car for your family might be a retail transaction. Buying a fleet of cars for your company may well go out to tender.

Key account management

At the heart of key account management is a power battle. Strong buyers will happily fleece weak sellers; sellers who are strong can dominate their channels. For instance, grocery chains are often merciless towards their suppliers. They drive down costs relentlessly. To regain power, the brand manufacturers (think Ariel, Mars, Kellogg's) create their own customer franchise, which evens up the power struggle a little. The big grocery chains have to stock the brands their customers want, otherwise their customers will go elsewhere. At the other extreme, the strongest suppliers such as Louis Vuitton and Apple dictate terms to their channels and will rapidly deselect those channels that fail to maintain quality or price discipline.

In key account management, you are the knight who has to fight this power battle: often, you will be left marooned in no-man's land between buyer and supplier, getting shot at from both sides. Some, but not all, people find this an enjoyable experience: the adrenalin rush can be quite a kick. Either way, key account management is the apex of the pure sales role: other roles become hybrid sales and management roles, as we shall see in relationship management.

Relationship management

Relationship management exists where the sale is highly complex and customised to each customer; where the product or service is non-standard; and where the customer remains with the vendor for a period of years. Typical examples might include high-end private banking, strategy consulting, even bespoke tailoring. Where key account management success is based on power, information and negotiating skills, relationship management success is built on trust, knowing the client and successful delivery. In many cases, the relationship manager is not a pure sales role: the relationship manager may also be responsible for delivering the product or the service. This creates tension because it is hard to be good at selling and good at delivery.

Key account management or relationship management?

Because account management and relationship management are often seen as the same thing, it is worth briefly exploring why they are very different.

An unfortunate fetish has grabbed the imagination of many people in sales. Key account management is seen as very last year; relationship management is all the rage. Next year's fashion will be strategic relationship management, because anything with 'strategic' in it must be good. Key account management is an art form in its own right: there are plenty of very good relationship managers who would not survive a week as a key account manager. My 'relationship manager' at my bank is very nice, wholly ineffectual and would be dead meat if he had to deal with a Tesco buyer. I would be able to sell tickets to watch the slaughter.

The table below frames the main differences between key account management and relationship management.

	Key account management	Relationship management
Products and services	Stable, predictable	Highly customised
Sales cycle	Short, regular	Long, infrequent
Buying process	Stable	Unclear
Key contacts	Purchasing	CEO, line managers
Access to client	Limited	Deep, constant
Role	Represent your firm	Coordinate resources
Sales effort	Mainly salesperson	Whole team effort
Nature of sale	Contest, power, negotiation	Win–win relationship

Occasionally, account managers are encouraged to become relationship managers. This shows a huge misunderstanding of the nature of the client. Account management is the stereotypical boy–girl relationship. The girl (vendor) wants a relationship: marriage. The boy (buyer) wants a transaction: sex. The boy will promise all sorts of things, but at the end of the day he just wants to screw you. Mention marriage and he will laugh or run.

The four sales environments

To summarise, the different types of selling are a result of how complex the sale is, and how frequently the sale happens: see the grid below.

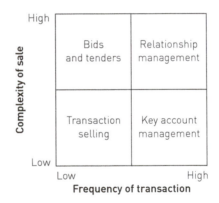

Different types of selling environment

Chapter 5

Key account management

At the heart of account management lies a power struggle. The more powerful side will always use its power to extract the most favourable terms. Usually the buyer is more powerful. When the vendor is more powerful, they are just as ruthless as the almighty buyer. Power corrupts.

Successful account management is the product of four main variables:

1 Select the right client.
2 Sell to the right buyer.
3 Build your power hand.
4 Negotiate well.

We will explore these four themes in the rest of this chapter. Because negotiations are so important in account management, we will put special emphasis on that section.

Select the right client

Selecting the right client is where we get dangerously close to putting the word 'strategic' into the phrase 'account management'. Picking the right clients is easy in theory, harder in practice; it was ever thus. The 'right' clients are the:

- largest by sales;
- most profitable;
- highest future potential.

Ideally, all three of these factors line up with each other. In practice, they rarely do. For instance, what do you do when faced with the following?

- Medium-size client, but highly profitable.
- Smaller client, but part of a huge client with whom your firm has extensive interests.
- Medium-size client, but with huge growth prospects if you are in with them early.
- Large client, but wafer-thin margins which will not improve.

I have found one simple way of answering all these questions: you sit down and argue for long hours with your colleagues about how to make the trade-offs. The important thing to do is to have the discussion: do not accept the hand you have been dealt. Just because you have been told these are the key accounts, do not assume they should still be the key accounts. Be prepared to refocus where it makes most sense. Your most limited resource is your time: you have to decide how to allocate your time best. And when you start thinking this way, you come up with more creative solutions, such as:

- Hiring administrative staff to do much of the preparation: freeing up more of your time.
- Partnering with your parent organisation to create a wider key account management programme.
- Creating a separate team to deal with the hi-po (high potential) accounts.

To understand the power of selecting the right clients, it is worth looking at a positive and a negative example.

- **Good key account management**. At Accenture we wanted to build the insurance practice. The first thing we did was to look at the market. For at least 20 years, the top 20 insurance companies all had the goal of achieving 10 per cent market share. This is the sort of mathematical impossibility that only actuaries could believe in. But it was clear that there was going to be industry consolidation: mergers and acquisitions were the only way some companies could achieve their growth goals. It was also fairly obvious who the predator and who the prey were going to be: some insurance companies were museums of management malpractice, whose survival was a miracle. The weak companies were easy to sell to: they lacked the discipline and the toughness of the better companies. So that made our choice of target very easy: we ignored the easy prey and went after the predators. As the predators grew, so we grew. The predators would not use the systems and technology of the weak prey. They would introduce their own systems. It was hard to get into the best companies, but once in we could simply grow with them.

- **Poor key account management**. In Japan we were working with a chemicals company. They believed in customer service, not in key account management. We counted the number of different grades of chemical which they produced: we gave up counting around 600. American firms in the same market would produce about 10 per cent of the variety that the Japanese firm produced. The grades were nearly identical, and in practice the buyers did not need such subtle differences, which cost a fortune to produce: each new grade of material required a changeover in machine settings, separate logistics, delivery, storage and billing. Most of the grades were unique to different small customers. A better focus on key account management would have enabled the Japanese company to focus more on the special needs of its top companies; variety and costs would have come down and profits would have gone up. When every customer is treated as a key account, chaos ensues.

Key account management creates a two-tier service, which is just what the key accounts want. It is also an easy way to alienate the rest of the market: you are helping the big boys kick sand in the face of the smaller players. The smaller players do not like that at all, and will be more than happy to drop suppliers who they see as not playing fair. So key account management has to live in a context: it has to be consistent with the same policies for the market as a whole. This is normally do-able: discounts, featuring allowances, trade promotions and special offers are all fine, provided they are based on transparent criteria, such as volume. For years the big grocery players kept on wanting 'special' deals from their suppliers: they wanted an offer that none of their competitors could match. This would please one buyer and anger the rest. Increasingly, firms like P&G have moved away from such discriminatory practices: they cause too much grief. Transparency and consistency count.

Sell to the right buyer

It is pretty obvious who you should sell to in key account management, isn't it? Well, yes. And no. The obvious answer is that the buyer is the person with a title like 'buyer' or 'purchasing manager' or 'acquisitions manager'. And for many account managers, this represents life in the comfort zone. The comfort zone may occasionally feel uncomfortable, when the heat rises, but at least it is familiar territory.

the buyer controls access to the two things you need most: cash and customers

Selling to the purchasing manager is classic 'push' selling. It is natural. Sometimes it is inevitable. But if you do this, it is like fighting with one hand. It puts too much power in the hand of the buyer, because the buyer controls access to the two things you need most: cash and customers. If cash is king, the customer is queen: the purchasing manager lands up being king and queen of the transaction, and you are left hoping for whatever scraps the purchasing royalty may throw your way. This is not a good place to be.

To even up the relationship, you will, ideally, reduce your dependence on the purchasing manager alone. When the purchasing manager holds the keys to the cash and the customers, you will always struggle. There are two ways of reaching beyond the purchasing manager, depending on the nature of the client:

- Understand the needs of other users within your key account.
- Build relations with your key accounts' customers.

As soon as you do either of these things, you cease to be just a 'push' salesperson. You create some 'pull' for yourself. Suddenly the power balance shifts. By doing an end run round the purchasing manager, you create a need that they can only fill by buying from you. The nature of the conversation changes, and should become much more pleasant from your perspective.

Two examples will show how creating pull can improve sales. By creating sell through, you make it much easier to achieve sell in. You have to work at both the selling in and the selling through process.

Selling soup tin labels: changing the customer

The world of selling labels for soup tins may not be the most glamorous, but it is instructive. It shows how moving beyond the purchasing manager to the rest of the organisation can transform your sales relationship. For years, a soup company and a label supply company had the normal, dysfunctional relationship between buyer and vendor. The purchasing manager, the buyer, was measured on the average cost of purchasing and he screwed his supplier down on cost each year. To make matters worse, he would then suddenly ask for special runs, short runs and bespoke runs of labels at very short notice and at the same price as normal. This wreaked havoc with the label supplier: each special order meant changing over machinery and complicated the whole logistics process. Costs went up, but prices stayed down. It was an increasingly unprofitable account, although it was a very large account for the label printer. The love–hate relationship was turning mainly to hate.

The key account manager was faced with the challenge of keeping the account, but making it profitable. The buyer had deep pockets but short arms: he had money but did not like parting with it. He was one of nature's true buyers. So: how to handle this challenge?

One day, the key account manager decided he did not want another argument with the buyer. So he made an unusual request. He asked if he could visit the soup factory and meet some of the people who used his product. The buyer was also relieved to have a conversation that did not lead to an argument, so they agreed to do a factory tour. As they went around, the key account manager asked each department what they really wanted from him, the humble supplier of labels. This is what he found:

- The finance department gave the expected reply: we want lower prices. Duh. But they did mention that the label supplier really was not that important: of every £10 of revenue, the label supplier represented about two pennies of cost. Every little helps, but soup labels were hardly on their radar screen. They dismissed him with a condescending wave.

- The operations team was pretty clear about what they wanted. They simply wanted to run a non-stop supply of tomato soup, with no fancy promotions, thank you very much. The longer the run, the lower they could keep their costs. All the special promotions, last-minute changes, test market products and niche products were a nightmare, which offended their desire for order and efficiency.

- Marketing pretty much hated operations. Marketing needed lots of special product, for test markets and for all the funky promotions they would dream up. They needed short runs for niche, but profitable, products and for export markets.

Selling endless tins of tomato soup was boring. The real action was around innovation, and that required flexibility from operations. It also required a vast array of soup labels, which they took great pride in designing.

● Sales loved talking to another salesperson, of course. And they were driven nuts by operations. One of their big problems was out-of-stocks: a sudden cold snap in the weather would send soup sales soaring and they would need to supply very fast to fill demand. Occasionally, marketing would come up with a winning promotion that would sell like hot cakes (or hot soup). Time and again sales would get the message, 'Sorry, we ran out of soup labels'. They would miss out on sales which were there for the taking.

The account manager and the purchasing manager went back to the office in more thoughtful mood. The conclusion was pretty simple: soup labels were a trivial cost, but had a huge impact on market performance. Saving less than two pennies on every £10 could lead to losing the whole £10 if they could not get fast and flexible supply. Even the purchasing manager worked out that £10 might be worth more than two pennies.

Eventually the soup maker and label supplier came to a new arrangement. They would still haggle like crazy over price for the standard tomato soup labels. But they also created a framework agreement for ordering short, emergency and bespoke runs to meet special needs. In return for fast turnaround, the purchasing manager was able to find some more pricing flexibility. The account manager looked like a hero for improving profits, but the purchasing manager also looked like a hero for improving the profits of his organisation: soup labels were no longer the constraint that led to lost sales.

So who was the customer? Clearly, the purchasing manager was the immediate customer. But he had a very narrow view of success. As soon as the account manager reached beyond the purchasing manager, he found different customers with different needs. As long as the purchasing manager had remained the only customer, the two organisations could never help each other fully.

Painting the customer: adding pull to the sales push

The paint industry raises a very simple question: who is your customer? It is the same question most industries face. For instance, in the grocery business the immediate customer is the grocery store: Wal-Mart, Carrefour or Tesco. But the stores are not the end customer: the end customer is the consumer. So you have a choice: you can build your relationship just with the grocery store and let them do the work of attracting the end customer. Or you can build a franchise with the end consumer as well, which is much more expensive but gives you power in dealing with the retailer.

In the paint industry, the equation is more complicated because the end users are more diverse and have radically different needs, as Figure 5.1 illustrates.

The needs of a decorator will be radically different from the high-tech needs of aerospace or of the automotive industry. Working through intermediaries, such as the distributor, does not work: the voice of the customer gets lost in the middle. If the paint company wants to stay in business, it has to hear the voice of the customer and start to work with some of the target segments directly to develop the products they need.

In some segments it is the job of marketing to create the end-user pull. Dulux has used the 'Dulux dog' for the last 50 years to build a consumer franchise around its paint business: how a shaggy dog has come to represent a paint brand so well for so long is one of those mysteries that is now lost in time. It is not the job of the key account manager to create an end-user franchise. But it is the job of the key account manager to make sure that the firm hears the voice of key customers loudly and clearly. This is the point at which the boundaries between key account management and relationship

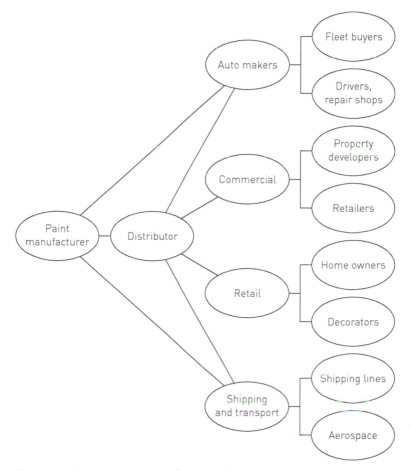

Figure 5.1 The paint industry (simplified): will the real customer please stand up?

management become blurred. The key account manager here is not just selling to the target segments, but helping to coordinate and integrate the capabilities of the firm to bring relevant solutions to market. The sales job may only be 30 per cent of the task; 70 per cent of the task is about identifying market needs and helping the organisation develop solutions. As ever, this is easier said than done.

Changing the rules

The two most common complaints I hear from key account managers are that they have to sell the wrong product at the wrong price. Your only consolation is that all your competitors are making exactly the same complaint: they will be convinced that you have better pricing and products than they do. As long as your relationship with the account is defined solely by the purchasing manager, these complaints will remain. And even in the best of worlds these challenges will not disappear. But these two cases show how you can change the rules of the game by changing the customer. Reaching beyond the purchasing manager (soup labels) enabled some pricing flexibility. Reaching beyond the distributor to end users (paint) enabled the paint manufacturer to develop new products and build market pull for themselves. If you can get beyond the purchasing department, you get a broader perspective of the client's real needs and you can find new ways of adding value and adding sales.

you can change the rules of the game by changing the customer

Changing your view of the customer changes your potential for pricing and product innovation.

Build your power hand

Shakespeare's Hamlet laments that 'There's a divinity that shapes our ends, Rough-hew them how we will'. At times, you may also be tempted to pray for divine intervention. But it is not divinity that determines your fate. It is power. Power drives the nature of the buyer–vendor relationship. The 'rough hewing' of the outcome is called negotiation ability, which we cover in the next section. Destiny is determined by the balance of power between buyer and vendor.

Power is not always in the hands of the buyer. When the vendor has the power, they are just as ruthless as the most powerful buyer. For instance:

- Louis Vuitton, Ferragamo and other luxury goods makers dictate pricing, stocks and layout to their retailers; any retailers who choose to object are quickly delisted. This is not quite the experience that most vendors have when dealing with Wal-Mart or Tesco.

- Auto makers control their distributors closely, with special attention to standards. In this respect they are like Starbucks, McDonald's or other top franchise operations; their franchisees may buy services, but the power is not with the buyer.

- Cartels, from OPEC through to the many illegal building and public works cartels, are an explicit attempt to build vendor power.

For you, the reality of power may be harsher. Real power lies on the other side of the negotiating table: with the buyer. The buyer controls the two things you most need: customers and cash.

There are essentially four ways you and your firm can change the power balance.

- **Build a customer franchise**. Even Marks & Spencer, which prided itself on its own brand, has finally succumbed to the logic of the market. About 30 years after the rest of the grocery trade, M&S worked out that if it did not offer TABASCO, Fairy Liquid, Mars and other iconic brands, then its customers will go elsewhere for their brands. It may hate stocking the brands, but it can no longer risk losing customers: it has to stock the brands.

- **Have a unique technology**. Dyson vacuum cleaners revolutionised the market: better performance allowed for premium pricing as well. Apple has successfully combined leading technology (iPod, iPhone) with a very strong brand franchise: it gets a double whammy. Selling Apple products into electrical retailers is not the hardest job in the world; instead of selling, most of the discussion is about maintaining price discipline, product allocations and featuring support. In other words, if you are an account manager with one of these firms you are in the driving seat. You are not so much selling as much as you are managing a franchise and a partnership.

- **Have a true core competency.** 'Core competency' has become abused as a term to refer to anything we feel is important. Go back to the original articles by Prahalad and Hamel, which first defined core competence, and you will find it is about a unique, company-wide capability that is competitive relevant. Firms like Valeo and Northern Foods have this: they do not have a unique technology (lots of other companies produce car parts or make ready meals). Their unique competence is around developing and adapting new products to meet the needs of their key clients (auto makers or grocery stores).

- **Be the lowest cost.** This is the death zone for many businesses, and they are driven there by customers always asking for lower prices. The logic ultimately leads to sweat shops in Vietnam and Guangdong, where very cheap labour, poor working conditions and long hours mean that they can undercut any UK supplier. Does anyone remember the UK cotton industry? It once led the world, and now exists mainly as heritage museums.

There is only so much you personally can do about this. The most important thing you can do is to pick the right company to represent. If you were a key account manager for a UK clothing firm supplying M&S, you would have a fairly limited career. You can no more turn the tide of globalisation than King Canute could stop the tide coming in. Working for Apple or Microsoft will give you an altogether different view of key account management, where you are as much a partner as you are a vendor. Remember the Greek curse: may all your wishes be granted. When you choose the firm to represent, you set your destiny.

In choosing the firms I have worked for, I have always asked:

- **What is their competitive advantage?** Do their competitors make the same claims, or is it really distinctive? In five years time, will they still have an advantage?

- **Who has the power: the vendor or the buyer?** Are we always fighting rearguard actions on price, or are we discussing how to build the business?

- **Will I enjoy working here?** What are the bosses like, what are the values? Will I learn new skills?

Of course, I have still made some spectacular misjudgements, but on average the outcomes have been good.

Negotiate well

Negotiating is the core skill that you have to master. The art of negotiation is much misunderstood in the public imagination. The public has images of politicians staying up all night to reach agreement on international treaties, as they indulge in an orgy of last-minute haggling and horse trading: making alliances, breaking them, destroying enemies and hopefully emerging victorious. As a rule, how politicians work shows how not to do things.

There are six basic principles of negotiating which you need to master. The other principles of selling, such as listening and being positive, remain true for negotiating. But these six principles are particularly relevant to negotiations:

1   Win–win, not win–lose, outcomes.
2   Interests, not positions.
3   Value is in the eye of the beholder.
4   Options, not a single-point solution.
5   The BATANA principle.
6   Intelligence and asymmetric information.

Win–win, not win–lose, outcomes

Sun Tzu wrote *The Art of War* over 2,500 years ago. He laid down three principles about when to fight. Those rules apply to negotiating today as much as they applied to war in China thousands of years ago. His three rules were:

● Only fight when there is a prize worth fighting for.
● Only fight when you know you will win.
● Only fight when there is no other way of achieving your objective.

Most battles inside an organisation fail at least one, and sometimes all three, of these three rules of war: they are pointless battles of egos, pride and politics. In the world of negotiating the third rule should be the motto of all negotiators: 'Only fight when there is no other way of achieving your objective.'

Many negotiating courses have macho titles such as 'Negotiate to win!' (always with an exclamation mark, and sometimes with capital letters so that the words shout at YOU!). There are several problems with the idea of negotiating as a war that has to be won:

● When you fight, you create enemies. It is harder to overcome an enemy than it is to persuade an ally.

● Even if you win once, you have doubled your problems for the future: your adversary will be twice as determined to win next time around.

● As the vendor, you do not have the critical resources that the buyer has: control over the cash and the customers. You are not set up to win.

Instead of negotiating wars, think of negotiating judo: use the other person's momentum and strength to your advantage. Work with them, not against them.

The win–win outcome happens when both sides believe they have got a good deal. There are two key principles to finding the win–win out of what often appears to be a win–lose situation:

● Convert positions into interests.

● See the value in the eye of the beholder.

Next we will explore how to use these two principles in classic win–lose discussions, which may start out as:

● I want to sell high; you want to buy low.

● I want to sell big volume; you want minimum stocks.

● I want a promotion; no promotions are available.

Interests, not positions

Position-based negotiating is like going to a bazaar on holiday and negotiating for a carpet you don't really want. The carpet shop owner will start with a price that is seven times too high; you haggle like crazy and get him to drop the price by two thirds. Good result, except you are still paying twice as much as it is worth, and you still do not really want the carpet. As in the bazaar, your friendly buyer may offer you a cup of tea when you visit. As in the bazaar, they will draw a line in the sand that will be completely unacceptable to you, such as:

● £23 a unit is final: not a penny more.

● There is no way I can take more than 50 units.

● Sorry, no promotions are possible this year. Wait until next year. Maybe.

These are unhelpful comments, especially if the line is drawn in the wrong bit of sand from your point of view. They invite you either to surrender quietly or to have a head-on collision. Neither of these are good outcomes. When a buyer draws a line in the sand, they are stating their position. In many ways, a position is like an objection: you have to qualify it and find out what the position or objection is really all about. Lurking behind every position there is an interest. You may not be able to do much about the position, but you can do something about the interest.

The first step to qualifying the position can be very simple. Ask 'Why?' And then shut up. Let the silence overwhelm the buyer. The initial reaction is often bluster, such as: 'Why do you ask me?' 'Because I say it is.'

Keep pushing with the 'why' question. The real interest behind each position is often obvious, but get the buyer to say it and to own it: if you say what the buyer thinks, they will deny it just to prove that they are smart and you are dumb. The buyer's interests are normally a mixture of the rational and the emotional. To take the examples above:

Buyer's position	Rational interest	Emotional interest
£23 maximum price	Maximise profits	Look smart to boss, meet authorisation limit
Not more than 50 units	Minimise stocks and maximise profits	Look smart to boss, don't get beaten up on stock figures at month end
No promotion	Need good staff	Avoid splitting up a good team

If we focus on the £23 limit, we go nowhere fast. If we focus on the underlying interests, maybe we can make progress by asking:

- How can our product help you maximise profits?
- How can we structure the deal so that it meets your authorisation limit? (Perhaps we can do monthly payments; salami-slice the pricing into different components such as product, insurance, delivery, etc.)
- How can we show that this pricing is great value to your boss? (Perhaps it is linked to some featuring or advertising deal where the vendor gets free publicity, etc.)

In the same way, when the 50 units of volume position is converted into interests, suddenly a whole new set of possibilities opens up:

- How can we arrange deliveries so that the order is staggered and stocks are minimised?
- How can we maximise your profits, given that this is a special promotion that will sell fast? Do you need a sale-or-return deal on this?
- Should we arrange the main delivery after your month-end stock check and do the big in-store promotion from that date, so you can sell all the promotion through?

The art of turning positions into interests reveals two more arts to master, which depend on creativity more than dull sales scripts. This is where you move ahead from being merely good to achieving excellence:

- Discover the value that is in the eye of the beholder.
- Create options, not single-point solutions.

These are the tricks that we explore next.

Value is in the eye of the beholder

Henry Ford revolutionised the auto industry by introducing the moving production line and other mass production techniques. The Ford Model T sold 15 million cars and swept away a whole cottage industry of craftsmen producing bespoke and expensive cars. Ford produced a car 'for the great multitude'. There was a price to pay: he let customers have the model T in 'any color... so long as it is black'. General Motors supplanted Ford by producing cars 'for every purse and purpose': they even allowed customers different colours. Changing the colour of the car was very low cost to the manufacturer, but very high value to the customer: it allowed them to personalise their car. GM saw the value to the customer which Ford did not see.

In similar fashion, all personal computers used to be black (except for some which were white). About ten years ago, computer manufacturers started offering computers in different colours and charging a premium for it. Nearly all the premium was profit: high value to the customer, low cost to the supplier. And if they could finally work out that not all cables should be black, then the wiring of the average office desk would cease to be an impenetrable mound of black spaghetti. Give the entire computer industry of brilliant engineers another 20 years or so and they may work out this source of customer value.

Value is not always where you expect it. We saw in the case of the soup labels that the buyer saw a simple equation: value = price. The rest of the soup company saw value differently: marketing saw value in getting short runs of special labels; sales saw value in getting emergency runs to deal with sudden surges in demand and to prevent out-of-stocks. Discovering value often requires reaching beyond the immediate needs of the buyer and looking at the needs of the organisation as a whole.

> value is not always where you expect it

Grocery retailers now measure value in terms of profit per square foot. But not all square feet are made equal. The area near the tills, where customers are often waiting, is premium real estate made for high-margin, low-price products such as sweets, which can be used as treats for the customer or 'shut up' gifts for fractious kids who have had to go shopping with mum or dad. Value can be more than profit or price. Stuart Rose, the CEO and chairman of M&S, finally abandoned the principle of only stocking own labels and agreed to stock 400 top brands from 2010 onwards. His reasoning was simple: 'Our customers were asking for these products, and if we do not supply them, they will go elsewhere.' Value is not just about immediate financial value: attracting and retaining customers is also a source of long-term value to any firm.

The search for value is not a simple formula: it requires effort to understand the customer – and some insight.

Options, not a single-point solution

Single-point negotiations are rarely productive. They are battles between two positions: higher or lower prices, higher or lower volumes, earlier or later delivery dates. As long as the negotiation is a single-point negotiation, it becomes a win–lose discussion, not a win–win. Given that buyers often have the most power, you are unlikely to win such negotiations. So the challenge is to create options – even where there appear to be no options.

For, instance, a price discussion never needs to be about a straight price point. There are always options:

- prompt payment discounts;
- featuring allowances;
- insurance, warranty and delivery;
- premium versus standard models;
- optional extras (colour choice, etc.);
- volume discounts;
- package deals.

The challenge is to stay in control of all the options: the pricing waterfall can destroy profits or make profits, depending on how well you control it.

Occasionally, it looks like there really is only a single-point solution. For instance, you either get promoted or not. This is where it pays to work through the ideas of value and interests versus positions to create some options and alternatives. I frequently help with the development of young teachers in challenging urban schools, as part of the Teach First programme that I helped to start. A common challenge is that they want promotion, but no slots are available unless either the incumbent dies or they move school. So how do you deal with the position 'I want promotion' against the head teacher's 'There are no promotions available'?

Start by exploring common interests:

New teacher's interests	Head teacher's interests
Seek promotion	No promotions available
Gain responsibility	Find leaders for whole-school improvement projects (behaviour, literacy, etc.)
Build personal skills	Retain skilled, good staff
Earn more money	Avoid unnecessary attrition and save on recruiting costs

A little bit of creativity avoids the single-point discussion around promotion. There are plenty of common interests that can lead to a rich discussion. In this case, the new teacher got to lead a whole-school project on behaviour management, giving her big responsibility and the chance to acquire new skills. And the head teacher retained a good staff member, solved the problem of the behaviour programme and saved costs on recruiting, while paying the new teacher more money. The win–lose of a single point discussion became a win–win discussion around mutual interests. And the new teacher quickly got promoted anyway, as her success with the behaviour programme made her a very valuable team member.

The BATANA principle

So far we have assumed that all negotiations are like a Disney movie: they have happy endings, where everyone lives happily ever after. Life is not always like that. Sometimes the river that divides the two sides cannot be bridged. It pays to know how wide the river is and how far your bridge will stretch. This is the idea of BATANA, which stands for 'best alternative to a negotiated agreement'.

BATANA can simply be your 'walk away' bottom line. You have to know this. Even CEOs often fail this simple test, precisely when it matters most. They make a bid for another company and suddenly they lose all sense of reason. They have their investment advisers whispering in their ear: 'Dare to be great'; 'If you wimp out now, you are forever a wimp'; and 'Eat or be eaten'. The thrill of the chase overtakes logic. Time and again, academic studies show that acquiring companies pay far too much: all of the gains go to the shareholders who sold out. The best antidote to avaricious investment bankers is a used envelope. On the back of that envelope the CEO should, before the bid battle starts, write down the 'walk away' price: the maximum they will pay. That is a very simple version of BATANA.

In managing key accounts, BATANA can be contentious. You will probably find yourself caught between two overwhelming forces:

- The imperative to keep the account and sell volume at all costs.
- The imperative to make profits.

Where there is no clear BATANA, disaster ensues. The first imperative (keep the account at all costs) dominates. The buyer grinds prices further and further down until you are selling at marginal cost: the sale is making no contribution to overhead costs, new products, marketing or development. This means that either all the other accounts have to be over-priced and uncompetitive, or that the business as a whole slowly slides into bankruptcy. BATANA is the bottom line that keeps the firm from going bust.

Ideally, BATANA means having more than one option. If your options are 'sell to this client or you are out of business' then you are in a very weak position. If, instead, you have a portfolio of clients, then you are in a much stronger position. For instance, a large supermarket chain can make and break suppliers. A supermarket giant is attractive to suppliers in the same way that a Venus' Flytrap is attractive to flies: highly alluring and 100 per cent deadly. When a supplier becomes dependent on a supermarket giant, it usually has no BATANA: it cannot walk away. Some smaller suppliers have worked this out and refuse to let their sales to supermarkets become more than 20 per cent of their business. They lose out on volume, but retain a stable and profitable business in return.

At its simplest, have more than one buyer. When I decided to start a bank, I did not negotiate with one potential partner. I explored options with eight potential partners: I gave myself options. When the young teachers are exploring the opportunity for promotion, it looks like they only have one buyer: their head teacher. The smart ones test the market and start exploring options with other schools. They go from having a weak BATANA to a real BATANA, where they can walk away if that is best for them. A strong BATANA transforms a weak negotiating position into a strong one.

Intelligence and asymmetric information

Nearly all negotiations are based on asymmetric information. Going to your bank and asking for a loan is a classic example. You do not know all their credit scoring criteria, or what terms they can really offer, or what their costs and profit targets are. They know a fair amount about you, and will do their best to find out as much as possible to see if you are credit worthy. Lending money is easy, getting it back is harder. This is a basic truth which seems to have eluded most banks, with the result that we are now all paying for their folly in the aftermath of the credit crunch. They were lending with insufficient knowledge: offering mortgages with no required proof of income ('liar's loans') was an invitation to disaster.

The more you know about your customer and your competitors, the better placed you are. You are in the vanguard of gathering such intelligence, which is more than just getting copies of the latest price lists your competitors have left with your client. It is about picking up every hint. Normally, new product launches, pricing changes and big promotions get leaked well before they are formally announced. If you find your client is going for a nice golfing weekend, with your number-one rival, it may be time to start revising those sales forecasts and resetting expectations. Do not wait for the hit to come.

> the more you know about your customer and competitors, the better placed you are

The tale of the Saharan cabbage

Every scrap of information may be of value, as the tale of the Saharan cabbage reveals. If you were driving to a meeting and saw a field of cabbages, it might not surprise you. But if you were on the edge of the Libyan Sahara, you would be expecting to see dates, figs and possibly wheat. Not cabbages. There are two big reasons you would not expect to see cabbages:

- The Sahara is not a great place for growing cabbages.
- Libyans do not care for cabbage, and nor do their dogs.

▶

Being smart, you now start linking the cabbage patch to a few more factoids:

- Koreans like cabbage, which they pickle and convert into kimchi: kimchi is an acquired taste well worth not acquiring.

- North Koreans were rumoured to be exporting nuclear technology to pay for the Dear Leader's brandy habit in Pyongyang.

- The Libyans were rumoured to be trying to acquire nuclear technology.

You follow this up with a little satellite imaging and other intelligence gathering and soon enough you can draw a straight line between the cabbage patch and some North Koreans helping the Libyans build nuclear technology. Not exactly James Bond, but still a victory for British Intelligence.

As with intelligence, so with sales: every scrap of information counts. You cannot know everything. Insight comes from pasting together all the information from across accounts, and building up a picture over time. You need to understand how the client really works, what their decision criteria are, how you are positioned relative to competition; and be ready to spot unusual behaviour or to exploit seasonal trends.

Fortunately, you do not have to be James Bond to gather intelligence. There is a vast amount of information you can gather right now about your clients and competitors. For instance, you can get information from:

- Annual reports.
- Brokers' reports.
- Google: look up information on individuals.
- Social media such as Facebook: find out about key individuals.
- Company newsletters.
- Buyers: ask them what's coming up.
- Ex-employees of clients and competitors: get in touch and they will spill the beans.

- Trade shows.

- Industry magazines and journalists.

- Other salespeople: tap into the grapevine.

- Who turns up in the car park; who signs the visitors' log at security.

- What the buyer wears: their choice of watch may speak volumes about them.

- Your client's factory/office/shop: ask to look around, since they will often be delighted to show you. Find out what they look for, who else they use, who their customers are, and what the rest of the organisation really wants.

You need an insatiable appetite for information. Curiosity might kill the cat, but it makes the key account manager. Often the real insight may come from the most unexpected source. Unless you look, you will not find.

Chapter 6

Relationship management

elationship management' is a much abused phrase, used to make the mundane sound sophisticated. Administrative staff at my bank are given the name 'relationship managers'. Software companies even sell 'customer relationship management' packages, which are about administration, not about selling.

To simplify matters, this chapter focuses on one specific sort of relationship management: relationship management in professional services firms such as consulting, accounting, banking and law firms. In this context, the principles of relationship management apply to you if you can profit from sustaining a relationship with a client for years.

Look around the tops of professional service firms and you will find many rich people with fancy titles: partner, executive vice-president, CEO. There is a better title for all of them: salesperson. You can only get to the top and stay at the top if you can sell and sell consistently. The job of the partner is to feed all the hungry mouths that the firm employs. The partner has to have a stable of loyal clients who will regularly buy from the partner. At the top, you sell or quit.

Selling at this level is an art form in its own right, and is profoundly different from key account management. Relationship management has the following characteristics:

- Success comes from acquiring and sustaining relationships with major clients.
- Selling is not to buying departments, but to users, who are often in the C-suite: CEO, COO, CIO.
- Selling is a team effort; individuals struggle.
- Buying tends to be ad hoc, irregular and large scale, with no pre-set purchasing system.
- The product or service is highly customised to each client.
- The client is buying the reputation of the team and the firm, not just the promised service.
- You have to coordinate and integrate the efforts of the whole firm both to sell and deliver work.
- You do not just sell: you also have to work through the delivery of the service and be on hand to sell the follow-on work.

In most professional services firms you will find what you find in most sales organisations: the most productive executives sell four to five times as much as the least productive executives. This is not the result of fate, or of DNA and the accident of birth. It is the result of acquiring the core skills of selling and applying them to the unique world of relationship management. Previous chapters have covered the core skills, which you need in order to sell. These are:

- the logic of the sales conversation;
- the mindset of the success;
- the principles of selling;
- targeting the right accounts and individuals.

But there are also four distinctive elements of relationship management that have to be acquired:

1 Getting the first meeting.
2 Managing the client life cycle.

3   Sustaining the relationship.

4   Dealing with CEOs.

Building trust is at the heart of relationship management, but this has already been covered in Chapter 3, so we will not cover it again here. The other four elements are the focus of this chapter.

Getting the first meeting

The hardest part of any journey is the first step. And the hardest part of any sale is often getting the first appointment. If you work for a firm where you have regular clients and a regular calling pattern, this will be a mystery that you can happily avoid. For many other people, this makes or breaks their careers.

The biggest barrier to getting that first meeting is not the client. The biggest barrier is in our own minds. No one likes to fail. Even worse is the rejection by receptionists, PAs and other gatekeepers who prevent you from even talking to your prospect. It is a humbling experience, which gets no better with age or experience.

To succeed, we need a method for dealing with ourselves and for dealing with the prospect.

We all have our own ways of motivating ourselves to make the first calls. Here are a few of the ways that I have come across when working with some outstanding sales professionals.

- Find a room with nothing in it: no internet, no colleagues, no distractions. All you can do is make the calls that you have been putting off by doing other things, such as expenses, call reports and the administrivia of daily life.

- Set up a room with three colleagues in it. Have a competition to see who can set up the most first meetings in the next two hours. Share triumphs, disasters and learning as you make your calls. Use the power of peer group pressure and support to motivate yourself.

- Set a clear goal over a short time period (30 minutes or an hour). The goal may not be to get the first meeting, but to get an introduction from a mutual acquaintance, or to find the direct line and contact details of your key prospect by calling receptionists. Once you have achieved your goal, reward yourself with a break and a coffee, then set another goal.

- Play the No game. One colleague had a simple mantra: no is simply a prelude to yes. She believed seven no's made one yes. So if five people said no before the sixth yes she had beaten her own target.

- Be prepared. Have a script ready in your mind for whoever answers the phone (receptionist, PA, prospect) and for any eventuality ('Sorry X is unavailable'; 'Could you send some literature'; 'Give me your details and X will get back to you').

Everyone has their own method for motivating themselves. The important point is to do it. Now. Avoid excuses, avoid distractions. And the more you do it, the better you become.

Clearly, it is not enough simply to be highly motivated. You also need a method for getting the first meeting set up. Here are six basic methods that routinely succeed, especially when they are used in combination with each other:

- the personal referral;
- newsletters and content-rich insight;
- seminars and other content-rich events;
- public conferences and trade events;
- the letter campaign;
- the full-frontal assault.

The personal referral

By far the best way to get a first meeting is through a personal introduction: if a trusted friend or colleague suggests you meet someone, you are much more likely to agree than if a stranger rings up on a cold call. The chances are that in some way you know even the most difficult, important and inaccessible client. For proof of this, we have to resort to the Kevin Bacon game.

Kevin Bacon is a film star. The game proposes that no one is more than six degrees of separation away from him: the challenge is to prove it. This game was put to the test by the BBC in 2009. They gave 40 parcels to people around the world. The goal was to get the parcel to a scientist in Boston, Marc Vidal, by passing the parcel on to someone they already knew on first-name terms, who they thought might be closer to the scientist. From the depths of rural Kenya and elsewhere, it took on average six steps to reach Vidal. However, of the 40 packages that the BBC started with, only three made it to the final destination. That sums up the nature of targeted networking. We may only be six steps away from the person we want to meet, but knowing which six steps to take is very hard. We can expect to set out in the wrong direction more than nine times out of ten. The journey may be short, but it is not easy. Persistence is required.

The Vidal experiment was not a freak result. Microsoft examined 30 billion messages on its instant messaging service, used by 180 million people, and found that the average separation between people was 6.6 steps. The good news is that we live in a small world; if we work at it, we can find a way through to anyone we need to find.

> we can find a way through to anyone we need to find

The best source of a personal referral is an existing client. If you have done a good job for them, many will be delighted to pass you on. This is the most powerful way of getting the first meeting.

You should also build your personal network. Once people have met you personally, they will be much more open to meeting you professionally. There are plenty of ways of building a personal network:

- Join local and/or national business associations.
- Go to conferences and volunteer to speak (organisers are always looking for interesting and free speakers). As a speaker you will be noticed.
- Serve on the board of a local charity, church, museum or community group.

Building networks like these are not just about getting referrals. They also make you a more interesting person to deal with. It becomes easier to create rapport with clients if you have something to talk about besides work. There is even a risk that you might enjoy supporting the local charity, community or business group.

Newsletters and content-rich insight

When I landed in Japan we had an urgent need for sales. I spoke no Japanese. So how do you make fast sales in Japan when you speak no Japanese? For starters, you focus on foreign companies. But each foreign company is like a fortress: how do you get inside each fortress when you know no one on the inside, and very few people outside either? Start making yourself noticed is a good start.

We had to make ourselves heard. Tradition has it that foreign companies cannot succeed in Japan: it is a closed country. So we did some research and published a list of the top 100 foreign companies in Japan. We showed that half of them had sales of over $1 billion a year in Japan alone, and many were extremely profitable. We went from nowhere to being recognised as the experts on foreign companies in Japan. Closed doors suddenly started opening.

The tale from Japan tells a story: marketing must add some value to the client. The performance bar in sales is rising all the time. Perhaps 20 years ago you might have got away with some name advertising – just putting your name and logo out there. That is now just spam. If you want to get noticed, you have to say something that is of value. You have to give people a reason to take notice of you. For instance:

- **Training companies**: show you have a different and better approach; offer training tips.

- **Systems integration**: give case examples to show how you have saved costs and improved performance in the client's industry.

- **Strategy consulting**: share best practice from around the world in a regular journal; for example, the *McKinsey Quarterly* is very posh marketing and a chance for its consultants to show off to each other and, more importantly, to impress clients.

There are several ways of not using newsletters. Investment banks and fund managers tend to be past masters at saying the wrong thing. They all trot round to CEOs with essentially the same spiel:

- We are the biggest and the best.

- We come top of lots of league tables.

- We have all the answers (even if we do not know your question).

- We have done an industry analysis which shows that you must start doing acquisitions or be acquired.

- Are you a lion or a mouse: will you make the acquisition and hire us or not?

These bankers' presentation has the integrity of Pravda in the Soviet era. It is crude propaganda which carries zero credibility; and most of it talks about themselves, not about the client. But, ultimately, the investment banks do not want a relationship: they want a transaction where they get 3 per cent of the billions you spend. They are estate agents flogging companies, not houses; at least estate agents serve a useful purpose.

If you are going to use newsletters and offer content-rich insight, concentrate on your client's needs: boasting about your own services will impress no one except yourself. And the newsletters are simply an early stage in marketing and attracting new clients.

You need to follow up. Send a copy of the newsletter to each of your prospects with a short covering note, highlighting the relevant article in the newsletter. Suggest that your prospect might benefit from getting an insight into the more detailed information and work that lay behind the article. Do not assume that once you have sent the newsletter out that your phone will start ringing with clients desperate to engage you. They probably will not even see the newsletter. The newsletter is simply an excuse to make contact and to start the dialogue.

Finally, persistence pays. Make your newsletters a regular event: it may take six or seven editions before clients finally start to recognise it. Eventually, they will start to expect it each month (provided the content is good enough). By then, you are establishing yourself as an industry expert. Before that, your work may go straight into the number-one file: the waste basket or deleted items folder.

Seminars and other content-rich events

The World Economic Forum at Davos may not have had an interesting speech in the last 25 years, but everyone goes because everyone else goes. If you want to be at the top, you have to be there. You cannot recreate Davos with its ski slopes and power cocktails. You can do better. You can pull together the senior executives you most want to talk to at a seminar. For a good seminar event, remember four major elements:

- **Book an interesting speaker**. This does not need to be an industry expert. The speaker is your hook. It might be a top-name professor, or sports star or celebrity. If necessary, book the first person who pogo-sticked up Everest, backwards and naked.

- **Be selective about your guest list**. The other guests are the bait on your hook, so keep the quality bar high. CEOs like mixing with other CEOs: avoid dilution. If this sounds like high effort and high cost, it is. Cutting corners saves 5 per cent of the cost and loses 100 per cent of the impact.

- **Find an interesting location**. This does not have to be expensive. I have invited potential contacts to prisons, yurts and other unusual places. I am giving my clients bragging rights when they get back to the office. And most of them cannot resist the lure of doing something unusual which none of their colleagues have done.

- **Avoid too much of a sales pitch**. If you make a big pitch at your first event, you will probably find that it is also your last event. And avoid overwhelming your guests with your colleagues. In practice, your guests really want to meet each other. The ideal ratio is two guests for each host: you get to know every guest but the guests have plenty of opportunity to meet each other.

Your first event may get a few people: you need to keep on investing. Let the reputation of your events build. Keep inviting your key prospects. Slowly, more and more of them will come. The good news about this sort of event is that you are able to get to know your key prospects in a non-sales environment. You build rapport, and find out more about them. The attrition rate between seminar and follow-up meeting is normally very low: one leads to the other.

Public conferences and trade events

Conferences are of hugely variable quality. The variation depends on two factors:

- who goes to the conference;
- what your role at the conference is.

Most conferences are attended by mid and junior-level executives: if that is your target, then go for it. For big-ticket relationship sales, conferences are largely a blind alley – unless you have the right role. Even the humblest conference will work hard to get some big name speakers to appear. Offer a speech yourself; if necessary be a sponsor to get a speaking slot. Speakers will mingle with the great unwashed reluctantly, but will see fellow speakers as their peers. That is the opportunity to meet and organise a follow-up: do not try the whole pitch, which will only alienate your target.

Trade shows are different, and tend to be much more powerful than public conferences. The good news is that people who attend are self-selecting: they are likely to be your target group. The really important people will turn up on the preview day; anyone who has to buy a ticket to get in on a public day is probably not swimming in the right pool. On public days you will be irritated by consultants trying to get information from you and small start-ups trying to do implausible deals with you.

If you are going to do a trade show, do it properly. You need to stand out and look good. That means spending to win. Underspending is called investing to lose. And if you want to do

> underspending is
> called investing
> to lose

any serious business, make sure you have a private area for private meetings with key prospects. Your prospects will not want to negotiate in full view of the public and their competitors. In practice, do not rely on your key prospects turning up randomly and coming to your stand. Invite them before the event: host a reception or a seminar at the trade show and make a formal appointment with your prospects to meet them at an agreed time. This allows both you and the prospect to maximise their productivity at the trade show. Even if the prospect makes their excuses, you will have started a dialogue that allows you to follow up later.

As an eagle-eyed reader, you will have seen that something is missing from this mix: corporate hospitality events, such as sports events. In the UK, the summer season of Henley (rowing), Wimbledon (tennis), Chelsea (flower show) and Glyndebourne (opera) has largely been taken over by the corporate entertaining industry. Without corporate support, these events would struggle to survive. So there is a role for corporate hospitality, but it is not useful for getting first meetings. Corporate hospitality tends to be a way of saying thank you to loyal clients, and deepening and extending existing relationships.

The letter campaign

This is a version of the full-frontal assault (see below), where you soften up the defensive barriers with a well-judged letter. Done well, it is highly effective. Below is a real life example. I had to get an appointment with the CEO and chairman of a large bank. I wanted a billion dollars or more to start a new sort of bank. This was not easy, since I knew no one at the bank and knew no CEOs of similar standing. So this is the letter I sent:

> *Dear Mr xxxx*
>
> *I am writing on the advice of John Jones[1] who thought it might be of mutual benefit for us to explore a new business proposal. We are[2] developing a corporate middle market bank,[3] which can fill a gap in your portfolio between your successful SME and corporate banking businesses.[4] We expect the bank to achieve $50 million pre-tax profits within five years.[5]*
>
> *I represent a group of senior bankers who have been developing this proposal and can form the start-up team to bring this idea to market fast.[6]*
>
> *In the first instance, it will make sense for us to have an exploratory discussion[7] to see if this idea fits with your current portfolio and priorities. I will call your secretary[8] next week to arrange a suitable time to meet you.[9]*
>
> *Yours sincerely*

No hook letter is perfect, and it does not need to be. It simply needs to work. The letter above worked as a hook. The principles behind the letter also apply to a phone pitch or any other initial contact where you need to hook someone into an initial meeting. The main principles behind the hook in the letter are numbered and explained below:

1   This is the personal introduction, right up front to grab attention. The CEO knew and respected John Jones (an alias). The goal was to stop the secretary putting the letter in the waste basket immediately. Whether writing or speaking, you need to get past the first sentence. A weak first sentence leads to switch-off.

2   Note the positive verb. Not 'might' or 'hoping to' or 'thinking about'. We are doing it, the only question is who with?: if you refuse, your arch rivals may decide to be the partner instead. In truth, we were still at the hope and wish stage. But we had to show project confidence, not uncertainty.

3   Be very clear about what the idea is, so they see it is specific and they understand it.

4   Make the idea highly personalised to the client; be positive about their existing portfolio, otherwise you will encourage a defensive reaction and denial.

5   Size the prize: it is worth the CEO getting out of bed for this. It is not something for a junior analyst to look into. It answers the question: why should I bother?

6   Be credible: show there is support, momentum and commitment. In truth, the senior bankers were interested but were not going to give up their day jobs until a deal was done. This answers the question: do I believe what is being written or said? In other sorts of pitches, endorsements from bosses, clients, experts, sports stars can all work.

7   This is an easy ask: invest an hour of your time to see if you want $50 million a year. This is the first step of incremental commitment.

8   The CEO will not read this letter, the secretary will. Promise to follow up. When you follow up, the secretary will have forgotten about or ignored your letter, so be ready to resend it. Second time round the secretary will take it seriously because you have shown you will follow up, so the secretary will show

the letter to the CEO and ask for advice. The hardest task can be getting past the switchboard to the secretary.

9 Keep it short. The more you write, the more there is for them to disagree with or dislike.

Of course, the letter was only part of the effort. You then have to follow up because not only will the CEO not reply, the CEO probably will never even have seen the letter, which will have been binned by a PA who will have dismissed it as a crank letter from a nutcase. Be prepared to call and keep on calling until you get the appointment set up.

The full-frontal assault

This is what people think of when they think of setting up first meetings: making a series of brutal cold calls in the hope of finding someone who says yes. Pure cold calling can be soul-destroying work. In practice, the full-frontal assault works best when the prospect has been warmed up, with any of the methods outlined above.

Call reception and ask who to speak to: do not ask to be put through. You will probably land up in the desert of voice mail (do not leave a message: it will probably not be answered and will probably be seen as nuisance – as spam). Or you will get passed from one extension to another. Ask for the name of the person you should speak to and for their contact details. Then call them back directly and ask for them by name: when you ask for someone by name, you will get through. If you still have trouble getting through, try calling before 9 am or after 5 pm: this is when the corporate defences of reception and PAs are likely to have left. Your prospect is most likely to answer the call directly.

When you get through, have your elevator pitch ready: imagine you are in a fast elevator going a short distance with your prospect. That's how long you have to make your pitch. Focus on benefits to the client: 'I'd like to arrange a meeting with you to talk about a copier/machine/product/service which is typically saving companies of your size about £x per year – when would be a good time to see you?'

Managing the client life cycle

The first rule of client acquisition is: don't. Selling to a new client costs roughly seven times as much as selling to an existing client, and for good reason. New client sales have a high failure rate; initial sales are often low value; and significant investment is required in marketing and getting to know the client. In contrast, selling to an existing client is easy: you know the people and the issues; you know what they will buy and when; you know how decisions are made; and, hopefully, they will know and trust you.

So your focus should be to keep and grow your existing relationships. This is where you become more of a farmer than a hunter: instead of hunting out new clients, nurture existing clients. History tells us that farming civilisations beat hunting civilisations, although the hunters can have more fun in the meantime.

> your focus should be to keep and grow your existing relationships

But if a company never acquires new clients, it will run into trouble. At some stage, you have to add to your client portfolio to replace clients who disappear, and to grow the business. The scale of the challenge is related to the reputation of the firm. If you work for a top firm, such as Goldman Sachs, McKinsey or Accenture, then sales and marketing is relatively easy: in many cases clients will come to you. And even if you have to go to them, they will answer your call and open doors to you. If you work for a specialist organisation that has a less public profile, you have to work much harder to get the doors to open.

In practice, all firms need a simple sales funnel, which will look something like Figure 6.1.

Figure 6.1 Typical sales funnel for relationship management

The target is to move from Q1, the broadly defined market, to Q6: your stable of loyal clients. Like a proper video game, the challenges at each level are different and it is easy to fall out at any stage. In this game, Q stands for level of 'qualification': the better qualified the client is, the stronger your position.

What follows is a brief description of each stage of the process. We will then explore how you can move clients from one stage to the next.

Q1 to Q2: from the potential market to the prime prospects

Not all clients are created equal. The critical first step is to work out who you want to work for. Sometimes, this is a luxury you cannot afford. When I first arrived in Japan I found a business with no sales, no prospect of any sales and plenty of bills to be paid. Under those circumstances, any client was a good client. Working alongside the yakuza (Japanese gangsters) in Okinawa, or developing an interest in the potential for Norwegian cheese in Japan suddenly seemed smart. But if you are not desperate, it pays to focus.

The selection criteria are essentially a trade-off between potential scale and your competitive positioning. Ask yourself:

- Where is the largest potential?
  - Who will be the winners and losers in the industry we serve?
  - Which clients most need our services?
  - Do we serve the giants of today or the winners of the future, or both?
- Where do we have some competitive advantage?
  - Who do our competitors serve and are they entrenched or loose?
  - Do we have a special product or service?
  - Is there an under-served, under-competed segment: perhaps small and medium-size enterprises?

This is essentially a strategic discussion tempered by operational reality. Sometimes the answer is easy. When I went to Japan I spoke English, knew financial services and had my biggest sales in operations improvement. So – surprise, surprise – we focused on helping foreign financial firms improve their operational effectiveness, and geared our marketing to that. Sell what you can, not what you can't. Back in the UK, we took a more nuanced view: we identified all the potential winners in the insurance market and targeted them. As the market consolidated through mergers and acquisitions, we would be working with the winners, not the losers. The losers were easier to sell to, but in the long term it makes no sense to invest in losers.

The good news is that most of this can be done with fairly simple desk work, combined with some fairly difficult conversations within your team. It may be natural to chase what is in front of your nose; the discipline of giving up some easy wins today for longer-term sustainable growth is a deeply unnatural act for anyone with sales instincts.

Q2 to Q3: meeting and qualifying prime prospects

This is where the selling gets serious, and serious discipline is required. I have often seen a sales funnel filled with hope, not reality, at this stage. For a client to be qualified, it is essential that:

- You know who the buyer is – or more likely what the buying network and buying process is.

- You have a qualified issue that is important, urgent and has significant value if it is addressed successfully.

- You have price-qualified the client: they understand the scale of the challenge and the scale of investment required to address it.

- You understand the politics of the issue: what the hot buttons are of the key players and if there are any lines in the sand that should not be crossed.

- You know the key players and have developed some rapport with them: you know something about them as individuals. Ideally, one of the key players will be acting as your coach and champion.

- You know about the competitive landscape: who is competing with you, who the incumbents are and how they are perceived.

If you cannot cover all of the above points reasonably well, the client is underqualified and you will not have proper control of the rest of the sales process: be prepared for surprises, which may not be pleasant.

Q3 to Q4: managing the bid process

The best way to win a war is without fighting. The best way to win a bid is without competition. If you have got lucky or got smart in Q3, you will have found an uncompeted entry point into your client. Pile in, make it a huge success and build for the next sale.

If you are in a bid process, then remember that in poker, in Wall Street and in bids if you don't know who the fall guy is, it will be you. Bids are rarely fair. There is normally one bidder who is in pole position to win. They may even have helped the client write the bid, so that all the selection criteria will favour themselves. Managing a formal bid process is covered fully in the next chapter.

Q5: first projects

First projects often do not make money. They are used as a trial project by the client, to see what you can do. This is the moment to over-invest and put your best team on to the project. The first project is not about making money; it is about cementing the relationship. Think of each client as an annuity, a revenue stream. This is how credit card companies think of their clients: the initial relationship is unprofitable; the cost of acquisition is high and for the first few months the client may be able to pay zero per cent on outstanding balances. The credit card company is not trying to make money over the first few months, and nor should you in a lasting relationship.

Credit card companies forecast the value of each client as follows:

$$PV = \frac{(r \times t)}{(d \times t)} - COA$$

where:

PV = present value of the client

r = forecast net revenues from the client per year

t = forecast number of years the client will remain loyal

d = discount rate for the forecast number of years (t) of the relationship

COA = cost of acquiring the client.

In practical terms this means:

- Find clients in the most cost-effective manner to minimise the cost of acquisition, but set this against the need to get the most valuable clients who are likely to cost the most to acquire: gold card customers tend not to be acquired from down-market magazines.
- Maximise the net revenues each year.
- Keep the relationship going for as long as possible.

Push the maths and it fast becomes obvious that making money on a first project is much less important than building a successful relationship.

Q6: continuing work

These are the best of times, and the most dangerous of times.

You may think you now have a tame client. It is tempting to let the good times roll. You know all the power politics inside the client; you know what projects are coming up where and when, and it all seems easy. It becomes harder to resist the pressure of head office to jack-up prices, build profits, maximise revenues (even selling some marginal work) and letting the A-team players go hunting elsewhere. For a while, this works. And then the inevitable happens: the client recognises that there are hungrier players out there who will do a better job, and you lose your comfortable annuity. Only the paranoid survive: always treat each project as if it is a new client.

> always treat each project as if it is a new client

For the relationship manager, these can be difficult times. Relationship managers tend to get marginalised: 'We don't need the salesperson any more' is a way of non-salespeople saying that they want to grab their share of the action. Like a pack of hyenas, they will chase off the lions who have actually made the kill: they get to feed without making the effort.

In practice, there is an important role for you throughout. Your role is to manage the relationship, not to manage the project or day-to-day work. This means two things:

● **Keep out of the way on detailed delivery**. If you do not enjoy this and aren't good at this, you will mess up your relationship with the client. Share the delivery workload with colleagues who like delivery, not sales.

● **Focus on high-level issues with the client**. Ask: 'Are we addressing the right issues?'; 'Have we got the right team?'; 'Are there any problems we need to iron out?'

Effectively, you are in charge of quality control; you are the political fixer and insurance policy for the rest of the organisation. If someone messes up, the client can talk to you before things get out of hand. Few organisations learn how to handle this well: delivery people are so keen on their power grab that they may want to force you aside completely, or give you such a minor role that you cease to have any use or relevance. You have to stake out a clear role with the client that allows you to stay engaged, add some value and get the next sale.

The selling never stops in a relationship. In a typical consulting assignment the partner (salesperson) will be heavily involved at the start and at the end. An effective division of time is as follows:

● One third of the time on finding the answer.

● One third of the time on selling the answer to the client.

● One third of the time on selling in the next project.

The easiest task is finding the answer: leave that to the team. The selling task is the core effort. The best answer in the world is useless if the client does not believe it. So sell the answer. And sell the next project before the first one finishes, for several reasons:

- Once you stop, you lose the team.
- Once you stop, you lose the excuse to walk the corridors, find out what is happening, build relations and spot sales opportunities.
- Once you stop, clients have a nasty habit of forgetting that they need you.

Sustaining the relationship

Hunters and farmers have never got on well together. In 198 BC a remarkable treaty was struck on the borders of modern Mongolia. It is a treaty that speaks volumes to the challenges of sustaining modern-day relationship management. It said: 'Let the state holding the bows beyond the Great Wall follow the rules of the Shanui; and let the Han govern the state of the overcoat and hat which lies inside the Great Wall.' At its simplest, this is a basic peace treaty: we agree to stop killing each other and invading each other. It is somewhat remarkable for defining civilisation (the Han) by the wearing of overcoats and hats: they would find modern-day London or New York uncivilised by their standards. Perhaps they would be right.

More remarkable was that rainfall dictated diplomacy. The Great Wall runs along a line where rainfall is about 20 centimetres a year. Within the Wall, there is enough rain to sustain agriculture, which means settlements, civilisation and ultimately overcoats and hats or fleeces, caps and iPods. Beyond the Wall there is not enough rain for agriculture, so instead you have hunters, nomads and occasionally the Mongol hordes sweeping out of the steppe into China or Europe.

The 198 BC treaty is early, and definitive, evidence that hunters and farmers really do not mix well. They spend most of their time either ignoring each other or killing each other. That should sound familiar to anyone involved in relationship management. The hunters go out and build the relationship; the farmers then come in to sustain it and try to marginalise the hunters. It is a very uneasy relationship within the firm.

There are two ways you can resolve the tension between hunters and farming:

- Do both roles: be a hunter and a farmer.
- Stick to hunting (selling) and leave the farming (delivery) to others.

Each choice involves some compromise.

Relationship managers as combined hunter farmers

If you are a partner in a professional services firm, you probably have to be a hunter and a farmer: partners eat what they hunt. Each partner is a self-contained mini-business unit. The attractions of this are obvious: it increases accountability, performance is transparent and it stops senior executives retiring in post. The problems are equally large. Hunters rarely make good farmers, or the other way round. If you are like most salespeople, you may not be great at the grind of delivery, and delivery people simply do not get it about sales. And as business becomes more complicated and more global, it is no longer possible to have one partner controlling everything: selling and delivery is increasingly a team effort.

> selling and delivery is increasingly a team effort

You can succeed more easily with hunting and farming if the relationships you manage are relatively small-scale and simple. A good example is high-end private banking (not high street private banking, which is just a wheeze to make affluent clients pay more for their banking services). High-end private banking starts with clients who have a minimum of £3.5 million, or preferably £7 million of assets to invest: below that it is too expensive to create bespoke solutions for clients. At this level, you will know your client's families: you will go to their weddings, hide the relevant

assets following the client's divorce, be invited to their yachts and see the next generation emerge to waste daddy's fortune. The private banker both farms (delivers the service) and hunts (gathers new clients, often by word of mouth). And in the classic mode of the relationship manager, you will coordinate and integrate all the bank's services to deliver the right solution to the client. Private bankers may hunt and farm, but they do not hunt and farm alone.

The hunter farmer model also works if you have relationships that are, in reality, transaction based. Investment bankers like to claim they invest in relationships: that is nonsense. Investment bankers have relationships with clients the same way anglers have relationships with fish: they are there to make the kill. They want the next acquisition deal, the next debt restructuring, the next fund management mandate. The relationship is a series of transactions which are often competitively bid. In this world, it makes sense for the hunter to be the farmer: you want the expert to be leading the sale and also delivering the outcome. As with the private banker, you may need to work with the rest of the organisation and occasionally you will need to hunt as a pack to lock down a large or complex deal.

Dealing with a global client on a systems integration project which may last years and cost over £100 million a year is a different proposition. Heavy-duty lifting and delivery capability is needed to grind out the project: this is not ideal for you if your great skill and passion is hunting new clients. Trying to do the two jobs together is unwise. One generalist can do two jobs poorly, where two specialists can do each job well: that is the lesson that Adam Smith observed with the pin makers of Gloucester. Specialisation works. It was true more than 200 years ago in pin making, and it is true today in most lines of work.

Separate hunters and farmers

It is human nature to think that we are indispensable. The sad truth is that not only are we dispensable, we can disappear without a ripple. Most organisations are robust and have a keen sense of self-survival. As soon as one key player goes, others quickly fill the gap. Like Stalinist Russia, departing stars and tsars are air-brushed out of history.

If you have had a big success and opened up a major new relationship, it is easy to fall into the trap of thinking you are now indispensable. You may have a unique and personal relationship with the client. So it is natural to want to stay at the feast that will follow in terms of fees being generated. Human nature, as ever, is flawed. The reality is more mundane:

- Salespeople are not the best at the grind of delivery.
- Clients may like you, but they want the best person for each job.
- Delivery specialists will do better than salespeople at delivery, and increase the chances of follow-on sales.

There is, however, a role for you.

The starting point is to understand the role that you can play in the delivery phase: start at the end and work back from there. You play a vital role during delivery. You can be a combination of quality control and insurance policy. The client needs someone to speak to if things go wrong: it can often be awkward to confront the delivery people directly. If you are positioned correctly, you can be the keeper of the faith. You know what was really promised to the client, and can stay above the day-to-day fray. So you become the client's partner, helping the client resolve any problems and making sure the delivery programme is keeping to its promises. This also happens to be the ideal position from which to spot further sales opportunities.

The best way to achieve this relationship is to be explicit about it. Set expectations correctly. Tell the client at the start of the project that your role will be quality control alongside the client: set the expectation that you will bring in specialists to lead the delivery work. All clients quickly grasp this: they much prefer to have specialists than to have generalists. They will welcome the new team and you can quietly take a back seat. If the team is any good, the client will quickly hook on to them for day-to-day needs. Your challenge will be to stay sufficiently involved that you still have a relationship: if you only turn up when there is a sale in the making, the client will quickly learn to hide their wallet when you appear. Structure in a series of regular review meetings, or perhaps informal dinners, where you can check on progress, be a sounding board for the client and quietly find out what other opportunities may be emerging.

Dealing with CEOs

Why do people marry ugly millionaires? Because that is where the money is. Duh.

Why do people want relationships with CEOs? Because that is where the money and the power are. Duh squared. CEOs are to vendors what lights are to moths: they attract all the moths out of the shadows; occasionally a few get too close and get burned.

People behave in funny ways when they get close to money, power and fame. I saw Prince Charles make a visit to a school that I was helping. Hordes of flunkies appeared out of nowhere. They all stood with a rictus grin on their faces, hoping for a moment with the Prince. As soon as any cameras appeared, there was a subtle but vicious battle to get as close to the Prince as possible, so they could all get their trophy picture, next to their new best friend: the future king.

Most of the normal rules of selling apply, even in the C-suite. But here are ten extra guidelines to remember for succeeding with the CEO.

- **Remember that the CEO is a human being**. This can be hard to believe. If you treat your CEO like a boss, they will treat you like a subordinate.

- **Treat the CEO as a partner**. You are there to help progress their agenda, not just to flog your service. So all the sales rules about listening and seeing the world through the eyes of your client become even more important. If you use PowerPoint, you will be treated like any middle executive making their big pitch to the CEO. Partners do not hide behind PowerPoint: they talk clearly, concisely and to the point.

- **Be gracious**. Courtesy increases with power: middling executives tend to be more defensive, and have more need to prove themselves by beating up outsiders to prove their virility: this is low-risk compared to beating up colleagues. CEOs have less need to prove themselves: they set themselves apart by being more courteous.

- **Add value fast**. The CEO may be gracious, but if you waste their time you will find that you cannot get any more appointments. You will not be thrown out; you will be frozen out. The way to add value fast is not by bragging and boasting: you will not impress. The way to add value fast is by asking smart questions and by showing that you fully understand the CEO's needs, and that you can help the CEO.

- **Be bold**. The CEO is not going to waste time on a paper-clip usage reduction programme. You have to make a significant impact on the CEO's agenda, otherwise you will find you are thrown back into the pond of middle management to fend for yourself.

- **Be brave and honest**. Be prepared to challenge the CEO (in private). Few people dare to challenge a boss; so CEOs are surrounded by yes-people, which does not help them. If you are the one person who is prepared to raise an uncomfortable truth and avert disaster, you build trust and credibility very fast.

- **Build your network**. Never rely on the CEO alone: you need allies across the organisation who support you. The CEO's PA is a good starting point, if you want access to the CEO's diary. The CEO will talk to many executives, who also need to be your allies, since the CEO will be reluctant to impose your brilliant idea on their team. And when the CEO finally departs, it helps to be on good terms with their successor.

- **Always deliver**. Excuses are toxic and the 'I said, he said, she said, they said, so I said' discussion is a disaster. CEOs are always having to fight fires, and the last thing they want is for you to act like an arsonist.

- **Be positive**. CEOs are always dealing with problems and problem people. Do not delegate problems up to the CEO: take problems away. Bring solutions, not problems to the CEO.

- **Be loyal**. All leaders value loyalty, even more than they value competence. Failing to support the CEO and staying quiet at a critical moment, or going absent in a crisis counts as disloyalty. And, of course, never challenge the CEO in public.

Chapter 7

Bids and tenders

W ales were due to play against the all-conquering All Blacks in a rugby match. Before the start, a visiting dignitary met both teams and grandly announced 'May the best team win'. The quick riposte from the Welsh captain was 'Not if we can help it!'

Bids, like rugby, are meant to give every side an even playing field with fair rules designed to ensure that the best side wins. Life is rarely that fair. In practice, the effective bidder is like the Welsh rugby captain; you can do much to ensure that your side wins, even if it is not the best side.

Many salespeople I work with say they do not like bidding: it is too formal and too restrictive. This is not quite true. They like bidding, provided they win. They do not object to bidding; they object to losing. Effective bidding means knowing when you should bid and how to load the dice in your favour. That is the major theme of this chapter, which has three major sections:

1 Knowing when to bid.
2 Managing the formal response.
3 Bidding in the public sector versus the private sector.

Bids, like human beings, come in many shapes and sizes. Bids can range from a few thousand pounds for some work on our own house to multi-billion-pound contracts with governments. At risk of over-simplification, we will follow a typical public sector procurement process and show how you can load the dice in your favour at each stage of the process, which will typically look something like Figure 7.1.

Figure 7.1 Simplified bid process

Each stage of the process is like a funnel which starts with a large number of bidders and ends up with just one. Although the bid process is designed by the client, each stage offers you a chance to review your involvement, investment and strategy in the light of emerging information.

Clearly, there are variations around this. Simpler private sector bids might cut out half this process: steps 1, 2, 6 and 7 could disappear. Some massive international arms deals can take years to negotiate, with a huge amount of effort dispensed in the informal process around the fringes of this formal process. 'Informal' is a euphemism for the sort of skulduggery that generates great interest from campaigners and lawyers.

We will use the simplified process above as our core template, and note major deviations from it as we go along.

Knowing when to bid

Once again, Sun Tzu's three rules of warfare guide us on when we should bid:

- Only fight (bid) when there is a prize worth fighting for.
- Only fight (bid) when you know you will win.
- Only fight (bid) when there is no other way of winning.

We will deal with each of these three conditions in turn, focusing mainly on the second condition.

Only fight when there is a prize worth fighting for

This is normally fairly obvious. But sometimes the blindingly obvious can be more blinding than obvious: we simply miss the point. The core point is that each bid is costly, both in absolute financial terms, and in terms of opportunity cost: focusing on one bid means passing up an opportunity on another bid. So choosing the right battle is essential. The prize is worth fighting for if:

- it is a large prize;
- we are likely to win.

Clearly, there can be a trade-off between these two extremes. Bigger bids require more effort and may have reduced opportunities of success. Smaller prizes require less effort and in many cases can be semi-automated to reduce costs and effort even further.

You have to size the prize. The size of the prize is not just the monetary value of the contract. The other factors to consider are:

- What is the expected profit from the contract?
- Will contract variations be a profit gold mine or a bottomless pit of risk and expense?
- Does the contract help us to gain a new market, new client, or new service line?
- How desperate are we to maintain revenues and retain key skills?

Inevitably, these factors rarely all line up in the same direction. The result can be an intense political battle within the firm to decide whether it is worth bidding or not. The worst outcome is when the firm decides, half-heartedly, to bid. Like being half pregnant, it does not work. If you bid half-heartedly, you will be investing to lose. Only invest to win, even if that means doubling up your investment. Doubling your investment does not double your risk: it reduces risk by increasing the chances of success. The bid decision is an all-or-nothing decision: you bid to win or not at all. And if you bid to win, you have to put all the relevant resources behind the bid to assure success. In practice, this means that the deciding factor is often the second rule: only bid when you know you can win.

> the bid decision is an all-or-nothing decision

Only fight when you know you will win

If you don't know that you can or will win, then you won't: you are the fall guy that is destined to fail. Chasing a lost cause is a waste of time, money and effort, which most firms cannot afford: focus efforts only where you have a realistic chance of winning.

You know you will win if you hold at least five of the four aces in the pack. Bids should not be a fair contest. Unlike the Olympics of old, it is the winning, not the taking part, which counts. Review the following to see whether you are set up to win:

- You know the real decision maker(s).
- You know the real decision-making process.
- You know the decision-making criteria.
- You know the competition and are better placed than the competition.

By this point, many of you will be thinking that this is another BFO: blinding flash of the obvious. So let's look at the detail.

- **You know the real decision maker(s)**. These people will not be the bid managers who score the bid and follow the technical procedures. They will be the economic buyer, the top-level authoriser and the end user, who will all have their own agendas – which may be conflicting. You will understand their agendas, the internal politics and how to position your bid appropriately. For instance, public sector bids are painfully transparent and fair in theory. But if you know the relevant minister, have understood their agenda and have framed your bid appropriately, your bid will mysteriously rise to the top of the pile. In practice, your bid team should focus not only on the top buyer: you should cover everyone involved in the bid process, to minimise the chances of being derailed. (Organising the bid team is covered later in this chapter.)

- **You know the real decision-making process**. In theory, bids are meant to be fair, transparent and objective. And in theory there is no need for wars, famine and celebrity television. Back on planet earth, bid processes are rarely fair. The main causes of unfairness are that you should know the main power brokers (see above) and you should have helped determine the decision-making criteria (see below). If you have done these two things, then the bid process will be as fair as a show trial in the old Soviet Union: the mechanics of the process may appear fair, but the outcome is never in doubt.

● **You know the decision-making criteria**. In fact, you helped write the decision-making criteria, so that they are skewed in your favour. In most cases, the people responsible for drawing up the bid have less technical knowledge than the people who are making the bid. For instance, a firm outsourcing its IT knows less about IT than the specialists who will bid; a defence ministry ordering helicopters will know less about helicopters than the manufacturers. So they need technical help in framing the bid, and that help has to come from the bidders themselves. Each bidder will fight hard to make sure that the bid criteria are essentially a specification for their firm: you need to be part of that framing process. If you are, you might get lucky and have the bid framed in your favour. If you do not help frame the bid, you will find yourself looking at a bid that looks impossible to win. And it will be impossible to win – for you, but not for your competition.

● **You know the competition and are better placed than the competition**. Any remaining competitors are either irrelevant or you have brought them into your consortium to bid with you. Perhaps the easiest way to deal with the competition is to make them your allies. This leads straight to the next section, which is that the best way to win is to win without fighting. If all your competitors are on your side in a consortium then you are unlikely to lose. There are, however, three main downsides:

  ● Consortia mean that each member wins small, rather than wins big.

  ● There is still a battle to be fought over who is the lead member of the consortia, and about who gains control and gains the most interesting parts of the contract.

  ● Consortia can be a nightmare to both construct and to maintain: at worst, the only people who make money out of them are the lawyers.

Only fight when there is no other way of winning

Often, it is possible to avoid a bid altogether. The two most common ways of bypassing a bid are through:

● relationships;
● crises.

A couple of real life examples will serve to illustrate the point.

Two life insurance companies entered a multi-billion-pound merger. The main cost of the merger, which would lead to the main cost savings, would be the integration of their respective IT systems. There were many vendors involved, high complexity, high stakes and many ways of achieving the desired outcome. It was a situation that appeared tailor-made for a bid: set each vendor against each other and see who could come up with the best bid.

At the end of the first board meeting, the IT director of the newly merged firm calmly announced that he wanted approval for the new IT integration plan. It was nodded through by the other top executives, who were IT illiterate and dared not challenge the IT director. So much for the bid process. With that one decision, thousands of jobs were lost, several IT contractors were kicked out and one IT contractor got to be very happy. And it was not an accident. The winning IT company had targeted life companies that were likely to be industry winners. They wanted to grow with their clients, especially through mergers and acquisitions activity. And so they had been working with the IT director to develop a rapid IT integration plan: when the merger came along, he was ready to strike. He looked like a hero and the IT contractor got all the business. The relationship and the need for speed trumped the niceties of a formal bid process.

In the second example, it was a crisis that enabled the bid process to be avoided. We were facing the need to bid to government for the services that we had created and built: the bid could penalise our enterprise by putting us out of business. That's government for you. And then we got a call from the Prime Minister's office on a Thursday evening, which went roughly like this:

> Civil servant: 'I thought you might like to know that the Prime Minister is going to announce a major expansion of your programme on Monday.'
>
> CEO (as salesperson-in-chief): 'No, he's not.'
>
> Civil servant: 'I don't think you understand ... the *Prime Minister* is going to announce ...'
>
> CEO: 'No, he won't.'
>
> Civil servant: 'Let me explain this very clearly ... the PRIME MINISTER wants ...'
>
> CEO: 'I don't care. It's not his programme and we don't have the money. So we can't expand.'

The conversation went round in pretty circles for a while longer. The civil servant could not believe that anyone would say no to God, let alone to the Prime Minister. It was unheard of. And we did not have the money to expand, so no was the easiest word to say. A note of panic slowly crept into the civil servant's voice as he realised that no really meant no: there are few ways that any civil servant can commit career suicide, but telling the Prime Minister that he cannot make his speech is a particularly ugly and unpleasant form of career death. So eventually he did the only thing he could do. He asked 'How much [will it take for you to say yes]?'

So much for the bid process. By the end of a tense weekend of negotiations we had seven years of funding and the Prime Minister had his speech. We were the only people who listened, which made it an expensive speech. *Carpe diem*: seize the day (or moment) and make the most of a crisis.

Managing the formal response

Let us assume that you have not been able to avoid the bid, and that a formal bidding process has started. We now need to manage each stage of the bid process. As shown earlier, the bid process in a public sector bid may look something like Figure 7.1 (see page 192). Most private sector bids are shorter: they have more flexibility and fewer steps. In both sectors, however, the principles remain the same. We will look at each step of the bid process in turn.

1 Tender announcement

By the time the tender is announced you should already have a good idea of whether you want to bid and whether you are likely to win. Ideally, you will have had a role in framing the tender and will have been expecting its announcement. If the announcement is a surprise, you are probably an outsider in the bid race. So this is the point at which you have to make the go or no-go decision. If you go for it, invest fully in the bid. That means putting a bid team in place, based on three key roles:

- **Bid leader**. Responsible for the overall bid process, the bid leader (on the sales side) should know the key decision makers at the client (buying) organisation. These decision makers are likely to exist several levels above the procurement managers. Procurement managers often take a narrow and inflexible view of what is required, since they will be driven by the bid process and procedures. In contrast, the key decision makers will have a much clearer picture of what is really required and will be driven more by outcomes than by policies and procedures. The bid leader is likely to be involved part time, but has an essential role in making sure the bid is properly supported with the right budget and the right team. If the bid leader cannot get the A team to work on the bid, that is a sure sign that the bid is not being treated as a priority and is likely to fail: time to walk away.

- **Bid managers**. These managers are responsible for coordinating the efforts of the team, ensuring the bid documents are pulled together properly, managing the bid budget and determining priorities on a day-to-day basis. Bid managers will also make it their job to get to know the procurement managers in the client organisation. These are the middle-level executives who oversee the bid process day-to-day; they have limited power to make things happen, but they have unlimited power to stop things happening and to obstruct you. They cannot say yes but they can say no: it is essential to get them on board. If the bid is remotely important, then the bid manager will work full time on the bid. This has the advantage of paranoia: the bid manager will quickly realise that success is non-optional and will become committed, creative and paranoid about ensuring success. Part-time bid managers can hedge their bets and are less dependent on success.

● **Analysts and specialists**. These people do the heavy lifting on the bid: they provide all the technical detail that the bid documents will require. Ideally, they should be people who have an interest in the outcome of the bid: they are likely to work on the contract if it succeeds. When they have their own money at stake, they will go the extra mile to make sure that the bid meets and exceeds expectations. If they are part time and have no interest in the bid outcome, they will find it hard to put in the level of effort required for success.

Clearly, the size of the team will vary. It can be a few people putting in a few days' effort for a small bid, all the way through to a large team working full time and spending millions of pounds for a major defence or aerospace contract.

2 Pre-qualification questionnaire

This is where the buyer qualifies the bidder. The pre-qualification questionnaire (PQQ) is also the last chance for you to qualify the buyer and decide if this is an opportunity that is worth going for. There should be enough information in the PQQ for you to see if the specifications suit you, or whether they have been written by a competitor to freeze you out.

The PQQ is a bit like submitting a CV when you are job hunting: you cannot win with the PQQ or the CV, but you can lose. It is a purely mechanical process in which you have to show that you meet the criteria that have been set out. This will tend to focus on the relevant skills, experience and track record of your organisation. As with a CV, a little creativity in interpreting your experience may be required: your objective is to show that you have enough relevant experience so that the buyer can tick the appropriate boxes and you can get to the next phase.

Critically, you will also see how the bid is being managed. Often bids may be broken down into smaller lots, with different timings and budgets attached to each lot. If you have managed to influence the design of the PQQ, the breakdown of the bid should enable you to win the lots you most want, while leaving others to pick up the pieces you do not want. If the PQQ creates lots that do not suit you, it is too late for you to change things, at least in the public sector.

Once you have a view of the PQQ, you will need to decide whether to bid alone or to build a consortium. Typically, you will have very little time to build this consortium. Fortunately, your potential partners will be in exactly the same situation and will understand the urgency. You will know who your ideal partners are. In practice, ideal partners often select themselves: they are the ones who are willing to do business and talk. If a potential partner is slow to respond or has unreasonable demands, that is a sure sign that either:

- they are not bidding;
- they are bidding by themselves;
- they are building a rival consortium.

Do not waste time trying to dance with a partner who does not want to dance. Find a partner who wants to get up and go with you.

The main reasons for building a consortium are to:

- pre-empt the competition: make them part of your bid team;
- fill in any skills and capabilities gaps, so that you increase your chances of success;
- spread your risk on a major contract;
- align yourself with your customer's interests (for instance, subcontract part of the work to a firm in the country of the government that is offering the contract).

There are also powerful reasons for not entering into a consortium, which include:

- **Loss of control**. This can lead to battles over control and resources.
- **Demarcation disputes**. These may occur especially over revenues and responsibilities. These can be agreed when things are going well; they get nasty when things go wrong.
- **Commitment**. The lead contractor will be highly committed. However, the subcontractors in the consortium may not be so committed. They can be slow to respond or respond incompletely, which can be fatal during a bid process.

On balance, consortia are often last resort measures: they are preferable only to not losing the bid. Often, it can be better to lose the bid than to win it in a consortium. You need to qualify your consortium partners closely. Typically, the three most important things to look for are:

- **Trust**. If you know and trust the partner, then you have a chance of success. If there is no trust, then simply do not proceed. The greed of the moment may make you want to paper over the cracks, but the cracks will still be there and can open up at any time.
- **Track record**. Do your partners have experience of consortia? What do their consortia partners say about them? When

bidding, partners put on their best behaviour. But what happens later? Do your due diligence on your partners: if they fail, you will fail with them.

● **Clarity**. Trust can get you started, but it cannot take you the whole distance. The further you go, the more you need great clarity about who does what when, what the consequences of delay and failure are, and what the financial arrangements are going to be. These arrangements have to be formalised in writing. Assume things will go wrong: what happens then? Partnerships are easy to run in good times; the real test of a partnership is when things go wrong. Prepare for it.

3 Bid specification

The bid specification will come under many names such as:

● ITT (invitation to tender);
● TOR (terms of reference);
● RFP (request for proposal).

In the private sector, the bid specification is often the first stage of the bidding process: only the public sector has the spare capacity to indulge itself in the first two phases of the bid process we have described so far.

Private sector bids will tend to focus on four main items:

● outcomes;
● capabilities and track record;
● approach;
● costs.

In the private sector, you may well find that you have flexibility about how you submit your bid and how you prepare your bid. Use this flexibility. The most important task is the basic sales task: understand what the customer really wants. If the bid is worth it, invest time in interviewing the key stakeholders and all the main decision makers. They may not all be aligned. You can add a huge amount of value by helping align the executive team and clarifying what they really want. Dare to challenge their thinking. Most bidders take the RFP (or TOR or ITT) as a given. They fail to think outside the box, and the more

> invest time in interviewing the key stakeholders and all the main decision makers

junior client executives will want you to stay in the box, because that is where they are most comfortable. Only if you reach the most senior executives can you find the real thinking behind the RFP: that is where you can challenge,

shape and align their thinking. If you do this, then you will have converted a bid against competition into a consultative selling process. You will have established yourself as the trusted partner of the client and you will have built your credibility. You will be winning a one-horse race.

In the public sector, things are different. By the time you get to the RFP, everything is set in stone. They may be asking for an insane outcome using an insane process. But nothing will stop them. Once the process is set, the process is set. The main concern of the procurement specialists is to avoid a legal challenge after the contract has been awarded: they need to show that every step of the process has been followed to the letter and that the process was fair between all the bidders. 'Fair' in public-sector speak has a special meaning. It means that all the bidders are discouraged from taking any initiative, from deviating from the process or from doing anything original. The bidders, like the procurement specialists, have to follow the bid process to the letter. Never mind the outcomes: follow the rules.

In the interests of transparency and fairness, public sector bids will indicate exactly how many points will be awarded for different parts of the bid: this is the 'points for points' system. So they will award points for things that have little to do with the outcomes required: points will be awarded for the qualifications (not experience) of the team; for having a balanced ethnic mix in the team; for your work on managing risks; for your approach to project management. It is all verbiage, which you will do well to comply with. And the outcomes may well be judged on a value-for-money basis, where value for money looks more at outputs than outcomes. For instance, a bid for training services would look at the number of people trained per unit cost (value for money based on outputs). In the private sector, the focus would be less on outputs and quantity and more on quality and outcomes: to show how the training will help us achieve our business goals better. As ever, it pays to follow the basic discipline of sales: give the client what they want. If they want insanity and inefficiency, that is their choice.

4 Q&A or briefing session

Again, there is a profound difference between the private and public sectors here. In the private sector, if you want a questions-and-answer session, you will have to ask for it. It pays to invest and to understand the client's situation properly. If you make the investment in research and none of your competitors do, that is 100 per cent fair in the world of the private sector. If you work hard and your competitors are lazy, then that is a good sign of who should win the bid.

The notion of fairness works differently in the public sector: working hard and putting in the extra effort may not be encouraged because that would give you an 'unfair' advantage. With attitudes like that to hard work, it becomes easier to understand why taxes are so high. So in the interests of fairness, the public sector will make sure that everyone gets the same information and same access. If you ask a really smart and insightful question, then every other bidder will be given the answer as well. So the public sector positively discourages you from working hard, being insightful or achieving worthwhile outcomes.

In practice, the Q&A or briefing session serves two functions:

● **You can see who else is thinking of bidding**. This may also be your last chance to put together a consortium bid, if you see other suitable firms at the briefing session.

● **You can clarify some basic points of fact**. Often the lower-level official simply will not understand the budget and timing issues and will have got them plain wrong: get these misunderstandings out of the way fast.

Two things are well worth avoiding at this stage:

● **Do not try asking smart questions of interpretation**. It may only confuse the officials, and if they do come up with a smart answer, then all your competitors will get the same answer as well. You need to have done your homework early: you should have helped shape the TOR and should understand the meaning behind the verbiage.

● **Do not try to challenge or reinterpret the TOR**. By now the officials are set on a course and will not change it, even if they are heading in the wrong direction. It is too late for change.

The late entrant

Occasionally, you will find that you are invited to bid long after the bid process has formally started. Typically this will happen after the bids have been submitted and happens for one of two reasons:

● The buyer wants to screw existing bidders on price (but is not seriously considering you).

● The buyer is desperate: they are not getting what they want from the bids they have seen.

When a buyer wants another bidder to come in and keep the existing bidder(s) honest on price, it is unlikely that you will win: you are there simply to help the buyer screw the other bidders. You can oblige them by putting in a very low bid, which will have the merit of infuriating your competition. It may also help you longer term with the client: next time they may invite you earlier into the bid process. In the unlikely event that you win, you can always negotiate the price back up again as you 'clarify' the client's needs further. At worst, you can walk away.

The more attractive way of dealing with the late-entry request is to change the nature of the bid. The buyer has already established that they are prepared to be flexible over the bidding process; see if they are also prepared to be flexible over the terms of the bid. The goal is to make sure you are bidding for something on your terms which you can win, rather than bid on something where you have already missed the boat and are being invited to make a giant leap from the dock to the ship as it steams away.

> make sure you are bidding for something on your terms

We changed the bid terms effectively in the earlier example of helping a bank in Tokyo, which said that it wanted to reduce its costs. We helped it see that it did not want to reduce absolute costs: it wanted to reduce unit costs. That means holding (not reducing) costs as revenues grew. By changing the nature of the bid, we showed that we actually understood the bank's needs, unlike the other bidders who were mechanically responding to the brief they received. As a result we were the only runner left in the revised bidding race: even we could not lose a one-horse race.

The other reason that you will be invited late to bid is that the buyer is desperate. This happens. For once, I was on the buying side and was looking for a big training provider. The bids came in and they were rubbish. Unfortunately, this was just before Christmas and the contract needed to be settled in January. We were looking down the wrong end of a gun barrel. So we went out to tender again, this time inviting some targeted organisations to bid. We got lucky: they did not sense our desperation and we got a good provider at a good price.

If you are invited to be a late entrant, do your homework. Qualify the client: find out why you are being brought in late. The client will work quite hard to avoid telling you the truth: you have to work harder to discover it. As a late entrant, you have some flexibility to bend the rules. Ask to interview a range of executives, so that you can better understand the client and their needs. This will normally give you all the intelligence you need about why you are being brought in, the state of your rivals, who the real decision makers are and what they all want. From there, you can decide if and how to bid.

5 Bid submission

In the private sector, this is your chance to shine. Remember the basics of human motivation: greed, fear and idleness. Your proposal should work on these three themes, although not overtly so.

- **Greed**. Show that you will be able to achieve great outcomes, and that the outcomes are what the client really wants: this may be different from the stated outcomes in the RFP. Hold out an exciting vision which the client wants to achieve.

- **Fear**. Show that your proposal is low risk. No one will get fired for hiring you: you are a safe pair of hands. Quietly show that other approaches would be much more risky: create space between yourself and your competitors. One of the main fears will be around the team: 'Will I get the A team or the B team? Will the great people I see at the bid stage disappear once I have awarded the bid?' Deal with this fear as best you can: the truth is that often they will get the B team and that the bid team will disappear once the bid is won. Clients are right to be fearful. Fear is not just rational risk to the project: it is personal risk to the client in making the right decision. If you have built the right relationship with the client, this fear will vanish. If you stick to a purely rational bid, you will lose out to bidders who have a relationship with the client, even if you have the best bid objectively.

- **Idleness**. Make it simple, make it straightforward. The larger and more complex the client's needs are, the more important it is to make it easy. The client has many things to worry about: this is your chance to give them one less thing to worry about. So turn your proposal into a simple story about what needs to happen. Remember that a bid proposal is not complete when you can say no more: it is complete when you can say no less. Keep it simple and focused. You can always have detail in your 3,000-page appendix, if that is required. By the end of your proposal, the client should be able to say, in 12 words or less, why your bid is the best: give them a simple story which they can use on themselves and their colleagues to buy you.

In the public sector, motivations are different. The process at this stage is a purely rational process in which compliance is the key to success. You have to comply with each part of the RFP: you will earn points for each of the points required in the RFP. Put yourself in the position of the junior or mid-ranking official who is going to have to score all the bids. The official may never have met you. All they will be interested in is what you have written and how far your points meet the requirements of each stage of the RFP. The official will be scoring you against a pre-set score sheet and will require detailed documentary evidence in order to give you each point; the official will be paranoid about an audit check or challenge and will want to show 100 per cent compliance with the process. All this means you may well have to submit a mountain of documentation, very precisely targeted at each section of the RFP. You will need to follow their format precisely. You get zero points for creativity, flexibility or initiative at this stage.

In both public and private sectors, the bid document will need to be polished and professional. I have seen bids sunk because the bidder has not spelt the client's name right; they have got basic facts and figures wrong; presentation and layout has been sloppy. Just as people are judged on appearances, so bids can be judged on appearances. The most common cause of error is the desire to keep on making changes and amendments until the last moment: junior staff get over-excited about the bid and work overnight to polish it. The result is that they are drunk with

have your deadline
crisis 24 hours early

tiredness and mistakes creep in. Have your deadline crisis 24 hours early. Use the spare 24 hours to let the production people do a superb job on physically producing your bid: it is no good shouting at them when you have only given them 45 minutes to do a four-hour production job.

6 Interview

Inevitably, bids are not won by bits of paper: they are won by people. This is where the interview becomes important. And, for once, there is one theme that both public and private sectors hold in common: the importance of preparation. There are three questions you should ask yourself:

- What are the three questions I least want to be asked, and how will I answer them?
- What are the other questions that are likely to be asked?
- What is the message that I want to leave them with: why should they back my bid?

Beyond this, public and private sectors quickly part company.

The private sector is likely to be quite lively, with lots of challenges and many opportunities to shine or fade. It helps to have a theme, so that you can link your answers back to one theme ('We are about value for money, not just low cost'). Once you have a theme, you can move from being reactive to being proactive and taking control of the conversation; instead of mechanically responding to a series of disjointed questions, you can build a story which they can buy into. The private sector interview will be highly specific to you and your bid; it will move fast and change direction.

The public sector interview will, not surprisingly, follow a strict process. The interview panel (yes, it will probably be a panel and they will all sit behind a long desk) will have agreed to ask the same questions of all the bidders. And each person on the panel will be allocated certain questions to ask, which they will read out. And then each panel member will score each answer. They will not want discussion, they will not want debate. They will stick, limpet like, to their scripts, their score sheets and their roles.

It pays to play the game the way the interview panel wants it played. The first rule is the rule that all school children learn at exam time: answer the question. Do not deviate into other wonderful ideas. Give the panel exactly what they want so that they can tick their boxes and fill in their score sheets: make life easy for them. This presumes that you understand what the question is really driving at. If in doubt, you can ask them precisely what they are looking for from the question: this is likely to be met with a look of blind panic and they will carefully re-read their prepared question. The problems start when they have a question that is highly relevant to one bidder, but not to you. They still have to ask the question of everyone, and everyone still has to answer. Enjoy.

7 Preferred bidder status

At this stage, you no longer have to win the bid. But you can lose it, or you can decide to walk away. In the private sector you will not be told you are the preferred bidder, but you will know it because the client is still talking to you. If the client goes all quiet on you, it means that they are trying to tie down a deal with one of your competitors but are holding you in reserve in case the preferred bidder falls through. In practice, there is little you can do about this, other than keep lines of communication open and show that you are still alive, hungry and interested.

In the public sector, you will explicitly be told whether you are the preferred bidder or not.

In both sectors, this is where your negotiation skills become paramount. We have covered negotiation skills in depth already. The most obvious point of negotiation is price: the client will hope that you are desperate enough that you will cave in on price. Establish an early principle of 'something for something': you can reduce the price, but then you also reduce the deliverables, or the client has to offset your costs in some way, such as contributing team members to your effort. Do not be weak. As the bag of gold is dangled in front of you, it is very tempting to compromise: don't. They made you preferred bidder on the basis of the price in your bid, so price should not be a stumbling block for them.

> establish an early principle of 'something for something'

Although price is important, it is not the only thing to negotiate. In public and private sectors there are normally different things to look for.

Private sector negotiating points:

- **Price versus scope**. Make sure that any discussion about price is linked to discussion about outcomes and scope. Offer something for something, not something for nothing.

- **Timing and phasing**. Clients often want a security blanket. They want to know that they can opt out if things are not going well. It can pay to give them this opt out. The reality is that once a major programme has started, it is very difficult to stop without huge cost and embarrassment. It is a free give, which you can concede when you need a concession in return elsewhere.

- **Team composition**. The client will want to hang on to you and the bid team. If you have done your work well, they will realise that the best bid people are not the same as the best delivery people. Introduce delivery people early, so that you can make yourself redundant (if that is what you want).

Public sector negotiating points:

- **Reporting requirements**. These can be absurdly burdensome unless negotiated, so negotiate them and minimise them.
- **Approvals process**. Make sure that you do not have to get approval for everything you do. You will lose control and you will be bogged down in bureaucratic buck-passing which will stop you delivering on anything. Make sure you have control and discretion over how you deliver your contract.
- **Intellectual property**. For some reason, the issue of intellectual property (IP) always comes up and the client will always demand that they will own all your IP at the end of the contract. 'No' is a useful word to deploy in this context.

In both public and private sector contracts, make sure you have the right team negotiating at the right level. Often the details of the contract will be delegated to procurement specialists who may work closely with finance specialists. This is a recipe for hell: these buyers will be junior to mid-level officials who have little real understanding of what their organisation wants. They will try to prove their value by being 'tough' and negotiating 'concessions' while ignoring the bigger picture completely. Match their negotiating team with people of equivalent level from your side: let them sweat out the details. But make sure you stay close to how they are negotiating the detail.

At some point, inevitably, the detailed and technical discussions break down. The two sides of mid-level executives find themselves locked in mortal combat and neither is prepared to stand down for fear of looking weak to their bosses. This is the moment to step back in. Invariably, the more senior you go in an organisation, the more you will find flexibility and reason. If you do this well, the junior team will have isolated the areas of disagreement down to a few key points, and you will then be in a position to resolve them at a higher level. Do not escalate everything to the top: that simply irritates the client. Equally, do not get caught in the low-level negotiations yourself: you should be held in reserve as a big gun to resolve the blockage, when it comes, at a high level.

8 Contract award

In theory, this is the moment for breaking out the champagne. Hopefully, the theory is matched by practice.

> as soon as you sign, all the negotiations are over

But before signing on the dotted line and popping the champagne corks, there is one more job to be done: consult the lawyers. The moment you sign, you are legally committed. Put bluntly, that means you can be sued or you can go out of business trying to fulfil a contract that is impossible to fulfil. As soon as you sign, all the negotiations are over: you have lost all your flexibility and room for manoeuvre.

There is some debate as to whether lawyers, politicians, bankers or accordion players should be shot first when the revolution comes. But in the meantime we need to deal with lawyers and recognise that they have their value in the current capitalist regime. Make them work through the contract to make sure that you are not making any inadvertent commitments; they will be good at asking the 'what if' questions. Contracts need to be drawn up so that they deal not just with the good times, but also with the bad times, accidents and setbacks. When disaster strikes it is too late to hope that trust will get you through. The court will ignore who said what, where and when: they will look at what was agreed in black and white in the contract.

In practice, this means consulting the lawyers early. As soon as you see the draft contract, involve them so that you know what you should be renegotiating. And never be put off by 'standard' contracts. Standard contracts are no more than contracts that are drawn up by the procurement teams; inevitably, all the terms and conditions will be in favour of the buyer not the vendor, if the buyer is offering their standard contract. Just because everyone else signs a bad contract does not mean that you should do so as well.

Bidding in the public sector versus the private sector

Public sector bidding is an art form in its own right. In the private sector reason occasionally sees the light of day. This is not the case in the public sector, which has a logic all of its own. In the private sector the firm asking for bids is probably going to be motivated by profit and will probably want to see real outcomes from the bid, which they will weigh against the costs and risks of the bid. There will be politics, arguments and differences of opinion, but the basic logic of profit, outcomes, costs and risks will normally win the day.

Clearly, the public sector has no interest in profit. It should, in theory, have an interest in outcomes, costs and risks. But theory rarely beats practice. In practice, there are other motivations that drive public sector contracting. As ever, with anything to do with selling, it pays to understand the mind of the buyer. So let us take a short, but perilous, journey through the head of a civil servant.

> it pays to understand the mind of the buyer

There are few ways in which a civil servant can fail. The most painful way they can fail is by embarrassing the minister. This is an unforgivable sin, and civil servants will go to great lengths to avoid this. When civil servants talk about risk, they may appear to talk about the same things that the private sector talks about: operational risk, health and safety, critical paths and timing, and so on. But the real risk is personal: is there anything about the bid or the bidder that might embarrass the minister? If so, the bid dies. Let's look at two real examples of how this understanding of risk drives behaviour.

The time had come to save money. For the civil service that does not mean raising productivity (that requires cutting jobs, which is unacceptable). Saving money means cutting programmes. So which programmes do you cut? Well, you do not cut the big, bad programmes, because that would be an admission of failure and would embarrass the minister. You cut programmes that are easy to cut (even if they are good programmes). You cut programmes with low visibility. So you are running a good programme that looks like it will be cut. How do you avoid the chop? You make the programme so high profile in the media that the minister dares not cut it.

You have a programme that looks like it will be very successful. You want to sell it to government so it can reach scale and do good things. You have all the data to prove that it will be a big success. So it gets turned down by the civil service on the basis that it is 'too risky'. So what is your reaction? You could go back with a powerful presentation to show that there really is no risk and it will be a massive hit. If you do this, you may find you leave the meeting through the top floor window, not through the front door. You have misunderstood the meaning of risk. For the civil servant, the real risk is that your programme will succeed. If it succeeds, it will show that existing programmes are no good and that will embarrass the minister. So it is best to kill the idea. Instead, you have to go back to the civil servants and show that your idea will not compete with any existing programmes, it will be very modest and quiet and will embarrass no one. Idea sold, and you can now build your programme.

The further down the civil service food chain you go, the greater the risk aversion becomes. In the lower reaches of the service, using judgement is a career-limiting move: you might be wrong. Instead of using judgement, they use rules, procedures and policies. As long as everything complies with the rules, procedures and policies then no civil servant can be at fault. And they really like to have everything documented in detail so that they can prove that they have complied with their own arcane rules. This is catastrophic if you have a good idea that does not fit any of their boxes. It is wonderful if you are a scumbag firm that wants to rip off the public sector: as long as you comply with their needs you can get away with more or less anything. Remember, you do not need to demonstrate outcomes or profit; you simply need to comply.

As in the private sector, there is often a disconnect between what the top wants and what the front-line civil servants actually procure. For instance, the government commissioned some worthies to write a couple of reports on further education; to avoid embarrassing the minister, the civil service then decreed that they would take action on the reports and set aside £20 million for that purpose. £20 million is chicken feed to a minister, so the money and the directives gently fell through the civil service to a low level and were forgotten by the big shots who had other things to think about. By the time the procurement process started, it bore no relation to the intent of the original reports; it became a process-bound exercise that had no chance of delivering anything very much. Its only purpose was to show that the minister was 'doing something' about the reports he had commissioned. At least £19.5 million of the £20 million was wasted on consultants and advisers who got rich. ·

Behind all the noise and confusion over public sector procurement lies an eternal truth about selling: understand the customer and give the customer what they want, the way they want it. The fact that the public sector is so Byzantine and dysfunctional in its procurement process simply proves the point: you do not succeed by having the best product. You succeed by offering the customer what they want, however insane that may be. And remember, it's only taxpayer's money you are wasting. So that's all right then …

Chapter 8

Dealing with the tough stuff

Selling is easy, except for buyers, competition, colleagues, fate, bureaucracy and all the other hazards that stop us achieving excellence and achievement. In warfare, plans do not survive first contact with the enemy. In sales, our plans do not survive first contact with the client. Nothing is ever as easy as it first seems, which is very good news for you. If selling was easy, you could quickly be replaced by an abysmal automated outbound call centre. Because selling is genuinely hard, it allows you to stand out and to make your mark.

Anyone can learn the basics fairly easily. It may take time to master the basic principles, but there is no great secret about the basics. But to progress from being good to being great you have to know how to handle the unexpected and to deal with the tough stuff. Fortunately, most of the tough stuff is reasonably predictable. Although insurance companies cannot predict when floods or car accidents will happen, they can predict that

> you have to know how to handle the unexpected

they will happen and they know what to do in response to these apparently random acts of the gods. The same is true of selling. We cannot tell when or where challenges will appear. But we do know the main sorts of challenge that will occur, and we know what we need to do about them.

The ten most common problems I see and challenges I am asked about are:

1 Dealing with Mr Nasty.
2 Dealing with the competition.
3 Problems with price.
4 Qualifying for price.
5 Presenting your credentials.
6 Corruption.
7 Dealing with no.
8 Handling objections.
9 Using the telephone, email and the internet.
10 Professional guard.

Dealing with Mr Nasty

The customer is always right … ha, ha, ha. Many customers are confused and fearful; some can be downright offensive, rude and nasty. Especially on a bad day. And some buyers seem to have a bad hair day every day: they live bad hair lives and want to inflict their personal misery on everyone else. Salespeople are easy victims; unlike the buyers' boss, you cannot bite back. Mr Nasty takes great pleasure in abusing his petty power. He will happily goad you and then threaten you with no sale or reporting you to your CEO who, they will claim, they know as a personal friend. It is 99 per cent nonsense. And you have to find a way of dealing with it, short of hitting Mr Nasty.

The most important thing is never rise to the bait: never lose your temper or say or do anything that they can use to show that you have been offensive and unreasonable. You have to be a model of professional behaviour. Being professional is most important when the buyer is being completely unprofessional. What you think behind your face is for you alone. As one colleague inelegantly put it, 'Grinf**k the buyer': be sweetness and light to the buyer's face. Never let the mask of the professional slip.

So how do you grinf**k the buyer? Everyone has a slightly different technique which allows them to deal with the moment of stress and to relieve their anger and frustration. Here are a few of the techniques that I have come across:

- Imagine what your favourite role model would do in this situation and do the same thing. If your favourite role model is a cross between Vlad the Impaler and Darth Vader, do not use this approach.
- Become a fly on the wall and watch the event: as you detach you will be able to think more clearly and objectively, without getting emotionally involved.
- Imagine that Mr Nasty is wearing a pink tutu: it is hard to get angry with a fat 50-year-old in a pink tutu. Not laughing (or being sick) may be a greater challenge.
- Pull out your imaginary Uzi and splatter their brains over the wall; as the buyer does not know what you have done, they cannot even retaliate.
- Count to ten, just like your granny told you to. Let the immediate flush of anger pass and regain control of your feelings.
- Breathe deeply, as taught in Buddhist meditation classes. Like counting to ten, you can regain control of yourself and respond professionally.
- Focus on the outcome: where do you want to be at the end of the conversation? Work towards that, and avoid being dragged into the mire.

It does not matter what technique you use. The important thing is to have a technique that you can bring in to play at a moment's notice. Develop your own technique which works for you. When cornered, I remember Churchill, who could be famously rude, especially when he drank too much. Over dinner a grand lady accused him of being drunk, to which he replied: 'I may be drunk, but you are ugly. At least in the morning, I shall be sober.' The buyer may make life a misery, but in the morning I will be happy and the buyer will still be a miserable specimen. Happiness is the ultimate revenge: if you are happy, you have won.

> happiness is the ultimate revenge: if you are happy, you have won

Once you have control over your feelings, you can deal with the logic of the situation. This is where it pays to return to your negotiating skills. Move away from the bluster of Mr Nasty taking up a position: be clear about your interests, develop some options, be assertive (not aggressive or passive), know your BATANA and wear the mask of professionalism.

Dealing with the competition

The advertising agency decided to put their best people on to the pitch: they really wanted our account. They had impressive credentials and a good track record. But within 20 minutes of them arriving, they had blown any chance of gaining our business. They had used the first 20 minutes to do three things:

- tell us how great they were;
- give us their theory of advertising;
- show why their competitors were useless.

Part of the problem was that they had not talked about us or about our needs at all: they were boring us by talking about themselves. But their biggest mistake was to attack the competition.

They showed us, in horror, the disaster campaigns that their competitors had been responsible for. They implied that the competition was hopeless, and that only they could be trusted. Far from trusting them, we trusted them less:

- By running down their own profession, they looked unprofessional.
- Every firm makes mistakes: a more honest approach would have been to admit that they have made mistakes, and learned from them as well.
- Their competitors could, presumably, have done a very good hatchet job on the agency presenting to us.
- We did not want to hear them talk about their competitors; we wanted to hear them talk about our needs.
- If they were so rude about other people behind their backs, what would they say about us? Could we trust them to be discrete?

The more you undermine the competition, the more you undermine yourself. Putting your foot in your mouth and then shooting it is not the best way to sell.

But ... at some point you need to help the client make an informed choice. They have to know why you are different from the competition. The key to success is to focus on choice criteria. Do not pretend that the competition is useless at everything. That is more or less certainly untrue and you will lose credibility by suggesting the idea. They will be good at some things. You will be good at other things. The key is to show that you are good at the things that should matter to the client: you can say the competition is wonderful, but that they do best the sorts of things that are less important to the client. You do not need to say you are better than the competition. You simply need to show that your offering fits better with the client's needs.

There is a soft and a hard way of painting the differences between yourself and competition.

The soft way of painting the difference is to make the client think long and hard about the criteria they will use for deciding who to buy from. If you have listened well, you should be able to persuade the client to rate most highly those criteria where you have most strength. For instance:

- Initial price is important, but most of our customers tell us that they are looking at total lifetime cost/cost per usage: that is where we can help you.

- A programme like this is all about risk versus return: we focus on minimising the risk and maximising the ultimate return. The initial cost turns out to be a small part of the equation for most of our customers.

The slightly harder way of making the client focus on choice criteria is by saying the same as above, but making the trade-off with competitive offerings clear:

- Initial price is important, but most of our customers tell us that they are looking at total lifetime cost/cost per usage: that is where we can help you. The low-cost options tend to be attractive to clients who have low usage and for whom reliability and uptime is not essential.

- A programme like this is all about risk versus return: we focus on minimising the risk and maximising the ultimate return. The initial cost turns out to be a small part of the equation for most of our customers. Clearly, there are lower-cost alternatives out there – and they do very well for clients who can manage all the risk themselves and are confident of achieving the investment return themselves.

In each case you create distance between yourself and the competition, but without running them down. Hide behind the experience of customers and show what they think and why they choose your company or a rival company. By quoting market experience you are not attacking the competition directly: you create peer pressure to encourage your rival to follow the best practice of your rivals. You also set up choice criteria that will, hopefully, lead the client to choosing you.

The choice criteria tool is about making sure the battle is fought on your terms and in the way you want it fought. Once the client is using the right criteria, they will naturally gravitate to the right choice. Make sure the right criteria are the ones that favour you. This is particularly important for tenders and bids: do not wait for the tender document to be published. Work behind the scenes to make sure that the tender specifies terms and conditions that favour your offering: ideally the tender should be written so that it is essentially a specification of your product or service.

There is nothing wrong with competition, as long as you win. That means that the best sort of a fight is an unfair fight: make sure the choice criteria are all in your favour.

> there is nothing wrong with competition, as long as you win

Problems with price

When was the last time you heard a client ask: 'Can I pay you a higher price?' For the last 10,000 years or so of civilisation, buyers have feigned horror at the thought of actually parting with their money to pay for your services. 'How much is that leg of dinosaur? You must be joking! I only want the leg, not the entire beast!'

Here are four principles for dealing with the price problem.

1 Find out what the problem really is

When a client says 'too much' they might mean several things:

- The price is above their authorisation limit.
- They do not have that much money, right now.
- They can get a better price elsewhere.
- They don't think the price is justified by the value.

Before entering into the price discussion, it pays to understand what the client really means by price. Each case above leads to a dramatically different response:

- **The price is above their authorisation limit**. Rework the offer so that they can pay in instalments which are within their authorisation limit; or agree that this is the only obstacle you both face, and then get the authorisation required.

- **They do not have that much money, right now**. Offer some financing arrangements to avoid the problem of the lump sum payment.

- **They can get a better price elsewhere**. Find out what the alternative offer really is: it may be bluff or reality. More often there is misunderstanding: you offer a three-year warranty; competitors offer only one year, etc. Work through the detail; at very worst you will discover useful competitor intelligence. At best, you will get the sale.

- **They don't think the price is justified by the value**. Go back to the basics: what is the value they want to gain? Work the value equation properly.

2 Work the value equation

Value is not simply about price. Value can be thought of as a very simple equation:

$$\text{Value} = \text{Price} - \text{Benefits}$$

When a client says the price is too high, it is also a way of saying the benefits are too low for them. Any argument over price is a win–lose argument: no one feels happy at the end of it. So change the terms of the debate. Reconfirm what benefits are wanted. And then offer some alternatives: show that of course there are cheaper options, with less benefits. This moves the discussion from pure price ('I want to pay less') to value ('How much do I want to spend for how much benefit?').

3 Something for something

Once you anchor the discussion around value, not price, you can deploy the next principle: something for something. You can positively encourage the client to pay less: simply be clear that the result is that they get less. You can turn this around by offering more for more: more value for more price. It is in these discussions you can let the buyer achieve the psychological win: let them negotiate something that shows that they are a smart buyer and gives them bragging rights with colleagues and friends. In many cases, the cost of what you offer can be low relative to its value to the client: this is where the big win–wins are available. For instance:

- An extra year of warranty for free: minimal producer cost, potentially high buyer value.

- A free bespoke colour scheme: normal cost to the customer high, actual cost to the producer near zero.

- An offer to the trade buyer to feature this product on TV with your name: high value to the trade buyer, zero cost to the producer, who is going to run the advertising campaign anyway.

In each case, avoid simply giving away the value. Ask for something in return: the larger order, or the commitment to buy the premium model.

4 Understand your pricing structure: pricing waterfalls and pyramids

The pricing waterfall is a quick way to make money or lose money very fast.

To imagine the price waterfall, work out the price of a simple product: a case of soap. There are 48 bars of soap in the case which is priced at £24. Easy. Except we are now at the top of the waterfall and are about to cascade down it. From the £24 headline price we have to adjust for the:

- high-volume discount;
- in-store promotion allowance;
- media advertising allowance;
- prompt-payment discount;
- multi-line feature bonus scheme;
- customer retail coupon;
- coupon handling allowance for the store;
- temporary price reduction for the promotion.

So what was the achieved price on the case of soap? Did we make any money on it? No idea at all. If you are not controlling the achieved price well, you have a licence to lose money. Selling is not about giving product away; it is about making money. In the hunt to make the sale, it is easy to forget to make a profit.

If the pricing waterfall is the easy way to lose money, the pricing pyramid is a good way to make money. Buying a computer over the internet is an object lesson in how the pricing pyramid works: you start with a basic product and then work upwards. I tried this when I saw a good PC at £225. But then the extras started piling up:

- Microsoft Office suite pre-installed.
- Symantec security pre-installed.
- Upgrade the memory and hard disk.
- Upgrade the video card.
- Buy installation.
- Extend the warranty.
- Add a good monitor.
- Install a TV tuner.
- Did I mention tax and delivery?

Soon enough, I was cruising past £750: I suspect that the manufacturer was not losing money on all the extras. Many of the extras were low cost to provide, but high value to receive.

Both the pricing waterfall and the price pyramid show that there can be a vast gap between the headline price and the achieved price. The gap between the headline and the achieved price is where profit or loss is generated. The fog of pricing confusion helps one side or the other. Used well, you can deliver profit to the company and value to the buyer; used poorly, it gives away margin in an uncontrolled and unsustainable manner.

Qualifying for price

When should you qualify for price? As soon as possible, that's when. The same rule applies on the shop floor as it does in the board room.

When selling advisory services to CEOs, I had a standard introduction where I price-qualified them early in our first meeting. After the initial rapport building, we would be asked to explain what we did. The simplified explanation went, roughly, as follows (spot the price qualification):

> *We only work with clients where we can deliver significantly improved profitability through building revenues/reducing costs/raising quality [as appropriate]. What we find in working with clients in this industry [the CEO's industry] is that clients are currently focusing on the following three issues: x, y and z. When working on cost-improvement initiatives, we typically find that in this industry an initial investment of £3–£6 million should yield annual savings in excess of £10–£15 million. For example ...*

So now the CEO knows that he is dealing with a large opportunity, it may cost him up to £6 million and so it is probably an issue that he wants to deal with personally rather than delegating it to a middle manager. If we had done our homework properly, we would know that this is a reasonable target. If the client objected, we would focus the discussion on what challenges he faced and what the value would be of resolving those challenges: focus on value before focusing on price alone.

focus on value before focusing on price alone

The same principle applies on the shop floor: price-qualify as soon as possible. Do not waste time selling into the wrong price bracket: you will lose customers, sales and profits, and time by doing so. The simplest way to price-qualify is to ask: 'How much were you thinking of spending?'

The problem with this direct approach is:

- The client may well lie: they will tell you a low number so that they can be protected when a salesperson tries to bid them up.
- You have done nothing to establish what their needs are.
- You have established no rapport or trust.
- You put the client on the defensive.

A slightly subtler approach can work as well. If the customer is in a store and looking at a selection of computers you will note that they are not looking at all the computers: they are focusing on a few. They are already price-qualifying themselves through their actions. So after the initial introductions and rapport building you can turn to one of the computers they have been looking at and ask 'Is this the sort of computer you want to buy?' Their body language as much as what they say will tell you if the computer is a realistic option or an idle day-dream. This question not only price-qualifies, it also opens up the discussion about what they really want from their computer: you can establish their needs and wants.

Whether you are in the board room or on the shop floor, price qualification does not happen in a vacuum. Asking the CEO 'Would you like to spend £6 million on advisory services?' will yield a very fast reply and make for a very short interview. Price and value have to be linked from the start: no one wants to spend money. But they will spend money if they see they can get value from it. So you have to value-qualify at the same time as price-qualify.

Presenting your credentials

This is a great big, ugly bear trap. Even though it is an obvious bear trap, it is very easy to walk straight into it. The bear trap gets bigger as you deal with more senior people and more complex sales.

When we first meet a client, the client will naturally be thinking:

- Why should I talk to you?
- Why should I believe you?
- Why should I trust you?

The natural response to this is to present your credentials: show how great you are and prove that you are a person worth talking to. Sadly, what you say and what is heard will be two completely different things:

What is said by the salesperson	What is heard by the buyer
I graduated from Harvard	Arrogant little s**t
We work with over 75 of the top 100 companies	So will I get any attention, or will I just be a training ground for your juniors?
We have won many awards	So you are more interested in winning awards than helping clients
We are ranked number one	Not by me, you're not … anyway, they all say that

Talking about yourself is the bear trap. If you want to impress clients, the best way to do so is by showing you understand their issues and that you can help them. That means being able to ask smart questions about the client, not talking about how great you and your company are.

But this still leaves you with the problem of presenting credentials. The easiest way to do this is to send any relevant credentials ahead of time: qualifications, CVs, client testimonials, work experiences can all be put into an email or a brochure, which you can send before the meeting. It will probably not be read in detail, but a quick glance should demonstrate to the client that they are in safe hands when dealing with you. If they have any questions, let them ask the questions. But the more you try to present your credentials, the more you will sound like you are boasting and only interested in yourself.

In the retail world, credentials can be presented very easily on a business card, on the side of a van or on your letterhead. Any of the following will help:

- Membership of trade organisations.
- Established since … (only companies that do well survive).
- Over 100,000 satisfied customers since …

To prove you're good, don't talk about it: show it. Ask smart questions, show that you understand the client's needs and that you can help the client. When the client sees that you understand them and can help them, the need for credentials disappears as fast as snow in the Sahara.

Corruption

Corruption does not exist, does it? Well, let's try a test. Which of the following scenarios are corrupt and which would you never do?

- Invite the client out to dinner.
- Invite the client to speak at a conference (at the local Rotary Club, or in Florida with all expenses paid).
- Invite the client to a corporate event (a big sports event where they meet the sports people, or to a cultural event which they like).
- Make an introduction for the client; put them in contact with your old university, where they are hoping to send their children.
- Give the client some help in preparing a big speech they have to make.
- Offer the client the chance to test your product. (For how long and in what location? Take the fleet car buyer on a test drive in St Tropez/the Himalayas/Rio at carnival time?)
- Hire a sales agency to sell in country X, with a 10 per cent sales commission (the agency is owned by the brother of the minister of national procurement).

- Go through the express lane at Heathrow because you have paid for a business class ticket; pay an 'expediting fee' to a local official in country X to get through customs and immigration fast.

- Play a round of golf with the client (at the local public course, or at St Andrews on the Old Course with all expenses paid).

Reasonable people can argue that all of the above are corrupt. Others can argue that all are acceptable practice. Corruption is not quite as simple as law-makers would have us believe: and law-makers are some of the most corrupt people in the world. Most people do not set out to be corrupt: corruption creeps up on them. They start with some simple courtesies, such as paying for lunch, but then expectations slowly escalate. Gradually, we get used to the norms of the industry which require ever more lavish entertainment and incentives. Then, one day, the police call round with some rather awkward and insistent questions.

There are two ways to deal with the corruption issue:

- **Be very clear about your own values**. Each time you are faced with an ambiguous situation, ask yourself two questions:
  - Would my children be proud of how I have behaved?
  - Would I be happy explaining it to the police, who are going to put this in the most negative light possible?

  Beware that people's values can be easily corrupted over time. In reality, most of us rise or sink to the ethical standards of our industry and our colleagues. So that leads inevitably to the next method:

- **Choose your industry carefully**. Some industries are far more prone to corruption than others. The defence industry and arms sales are very problematic ethically. If you choose to work there, you can either be a boy scout or you can be successful: you are unlikely to succeed on both the ethical and success fronts.

Dealing with no

Often, no is simply a deferred yes. People say no to buy time, to provoke you, to see if they can squeeze you for better terms, to maintain a long personal tradition of being negative. Whatever.

But sometimes no means no: your client has just awarded the contract to a rival and no is a real no. You are not going to win the contract you have just lost. No one likes failing, least of all salespeople, who are driven by success. So how can you deal with no? There are three main ways:

Blame

Blame is the easiest way out. It is often expressed as:

- Our prices are uncompetitive. [Have you ever heard a colleague complaining that our prices are too low?]
- We have the wrong product.
- There was not enough support from marketing and ops.
- They were uncompetitive delivery times.

In other words, it is anyone's fault except mine. And if it is a big contract, the blame game can get vicious and career threatening. The blame game quickly goes nowhere.

Denial

Shrinks take pity on people who are 'in denial'. Which shows that shrinks probably should never get into sales. Denial is good, in moderation. If we beat ourselves up every time we had a setback, we would go nuts. And then we would need to see a shrink, because of our lack of denial. The denial mindset says things like:

- It was their loss, not mine.
- They made a bad choice.

- It was just not our day.
- There are plenty of other fish in the sea.

In my case, I simply airbrush disasters out of my mind. I know there are people who have seriously cheated me in the past: I cannot even remember their names. Uncle Joe Stalin would be proud of my ability to airbrush history.

Denial runs into problems where it prevents us from learning. Each no is an opportunity to learn how to improve.

Future focus

We cannot change the past, but we can change the future. The past is only useful if it helps us sell more in the future. So if we are to look back at no, it makes sense to learn from it. When senior managers say they 'want everyone to learn from mistakes made' what they mean is 'I want to find someone to blame and to humiliate in public to scare everyone else into working harder'. It is usually not a very happy conversation. Fortunately, there is a better way.

Instead, after every significant campaign (win, draw or lose) I pull the team together to review what happened. It is important to review successes as well as failures: we should build on what works. Also, it makes the review a natural habit, rather than an inquisition that only happens when there is a setback. I have three questions for the review:

- **WWW: what went well**. You do not succeed by focusing on and eliminating weaknesses. Sales stars and sports stars do not win by focusing on weaknesses. Focus on strengths: remind yourself about them and keep doing them. Staying positive is especially important when things have gone wrong.
- **EBI: even better if**. What could we do better next time around? Again, turn the negative into a positive. Instead of 'We have lousy pricing' try 'How to demonstrate our value

better'. The first statement gets nowhere, the second might lead to some creative solutions.

- **IWIK: I wish I knew**. This is about getting to facts, not opinions. Everyone, including the customer has opinions. Customers will tell you what they think you want to hear ('Your prices are too high') rather than what you need to hear ('I really liked your competitor after he took me out to golf for a day'). Never trust opinions: find the facts.

There is a trap with learning: you can do too much of it. If you review each and every call and you make 12 calls a day, you will find first that you cannot make so many calls, and second you will get completely confused. What works in one call may not work in the next. And you cannot keep on chopping and changing your style the whole time. The key is to look for patterns of successes and setbacks. Review each day, or perhaps each week: this allows time for patterns to emerge.

Handling objections

Selling can be as easy or as complicated as you want it to be. Dealing with objections is an area where it often gets very complicated. Which means that we need a way of making it simple: life is complicated enough as it is. I was taught a simple four-step method for dealing with objections. It may not be clever, but it works.

Step one: decide if it is really an objection

Negative statements and questions are not always objections. They normally fall into one of three sorts of response:

- a buying signal;
- an invitation to negotiate;
- a genuine objection.

A buying signal may be disguised as a question or even as an objection. Buying signals are when clients start probing the where, when and how of the purchase: they are not questioning if they should buy or why they should buy. They have already made that decision. They are now focused on the mechanics of the purchase. Here are examples of the different sorts of objection:

Buying signal objections

- You can't deliver then: no one will be in. [They want to buy, but they need a good delivery slot.]
- The problem is you send the smart people to make the pitch, and then you send in all the idiots to do the work. [They want to buy, but they want the right team to do the work.]
- Green is a terrible colour. [They want to buy, in the right colour.]

Invitations to negotiate

- You are more expensive than the competition. [You are being invited not just to talk price, but to understand the total lifetime cost/value and financing mix.]
- That service package is useless. [This is an invitation to understand why service is so important to them, what they really need and how to support them.]

Genuine objections

- Manufacturing will never let me buy this: it does not meet their needs.
- We currently have a supplier with another six months to run on their contract.
- That is attractive, but just too risky for me right now.

Step two: support the objection

Support the objection? Are you crazy? Aren't we meant to overcome objections? Eventually, you will overcome the objection. But do not fight it head on: the battle will be bloody. Use sales judo: use the momentum of the client to your advantage. Sales judo is the key to overcoming objections.

To support the objection all you need to do is to paraphrase it, in your own words and then say something like:

- Yes, many clients ask about that issue.
- I worried about that when I first started on this.
- That is a fair enough concern.

By paraphrasing, you confirm to the client that you have heard and understood what they are saying. By empathising with them, you show that you now want to help them: you are not going to fight them; you are not going to prove that they are wrong; you are not going to get into a contest. You will help them: you are on their side. They are now ready to listen and cooperate with you, rather than fight you. Sales judo is now working in your favour.

Step three: validate the concern

What clients say and what clients think are completely different things. Clients' mouths are not always wired to their brains. This step is about finding out what they think: getting behind what they have said. For instance, how many times have you heard clients say the following?

- I need to think it over.
- I have to refer this to my boss.
- We don't have the budget right now.
- Could you come back next week/month/year/in my next life?
- Could you leave us your brochure?

Clearly, none of these are the real objection. But before you do your probing, confirm with the client that this is the only or main concern. You want to focus the conversation, rather than have it ramble from one concern to another. Once they have stated that this is their main or only concern, you have some focus and direction for the conversation.

Each of the non-objections above open the way to some easy questions:

- **I need to think it over**. Fine: what is it that you need to think through most?

- **I have to refer this to my boss**. OK: what do we need to do [together] to get the support of your boss?

- **We don't have the budget right now**. Tell me how the budget system works: perhaps there is something we can do to help you.

- **Could you come back next week/month/year/in my next life?** OK [this is a required lie to make the client feel comfortable; you never want to come back next week: by then the lead will have gone cold]. What is it that we need to resolve over the next week?

- **Could you leave us your brochure?** Of course: what are you looking for in the brochure?

In every case you need to engage the client to find out what their real objection is. Validate the real objection as their main or only objection, and you can start moving the conversation towards a successful close.

Step four: answer the objection

Answer completely and thoroughly, and then confirm with the client that you have responded to their concern.

Step four is a huge trap that is easy to fall into. If you let step four become step one, you quickly find yourself arguing with the client about something that is not their real objection. The result is normally ugly. Even if you think you have the perfect answer, do not use it until you have been through the first three steps. This is sales judo, not a boxing match with points scored for each time you hit your opponent.

Step zero: the best way to handle objections

If a four-step process is too complicated, do not worry. There is an easier and better way of handling objections: the zero-step approach. The best way to handle objections is to pre-empt them. If you have listened well in the early part of the discussion, you will know what the client's questions and concerns are

> the best way to handle objections is to pre-empt them

likely to be. You can pre-empt them all as you explain how your idea or proposal works. As ever, prevention is better than cure.

Using the telephone, email and the internet

In the bad old days, nearly all selling was done face to face. Face to face is still the best way of selling: it is easier to trust someone we see. But even where most of the sale is being conducted face to face, an increasing proportion of the sale happens remotely: by telephone or over the internet. A combination of letters, emails and phone calls might be used to set up a meeting. And the same might be needed to follow up, confirm details and sort out logistics.

The good news and the bad news about non face-to-face communication is that no one knows who you are: 'On the internet, no one knows that you are a dog.' There are plenty of salespeople who do very well face to face, but struggle when they communicate remotely: their telephone persona is all wrong. This counts. Professor Mehrabian, in a classic study done at UCLA, calculated that our impressions of someone are formed as follows:

- What they say (words): 7 per cent.
- How they say it (tone of voice): 38 per cent.
- How they look (facial appearance): 55 per cent.

With the visual clues removed, we may well form a very different impression of someone. So we have to focus very carefully on what we say and, especially, on how we say it.

Telephone

We can learn effective telephone technique from two unlikely sources: journalists and Jaguar cars. When Sir Edward Lyons set up Jaguar cars, he had a motto that was meant to guide the development of every model: space, pace and grace. Space, pace and grace are good enough for making Jaguars and they are good enough for making telephone calls as well. Here is how they apply to making phone calls:

- **Space**. Give the client room to talk. Do not be afraid of silence, especially after you have asked a question. The mantra of 'Two ears, one mouth and use them in that proportion' applies as much to phone meetings as they do to face-to-face meetings.

- **Pace**. Go slow. If something is important, the best way to give it emphasis is to slow down. Raising your voice is just heckling, and the client cannot see your body gestures which show that what you are saying is important. If you listen to Martin Luther King's 'I have a dream …' speech you will find he spoke just 128 words in a minute. Weak salespeople feel they need to get their pitch in before being cut off, so will talk at over 200 words a minute. They sound like leprechauns on speed and impress no one but themselves.

- **Grace**. Telephones are treated as transaction machines, not relationship machines. People tend to be short and sharp. A little courtesy goes a long way. At minimum, if the call is important treat it like a proper meeting. Be in a quiet room where you are not distracted. If you call from an airport or a café, you will sound wrong and the background will sound wrong.

There is one more trick which we can learn, from journalists. Trainee journalists have basic telephone etiquette hammered into them when they start. A few of the basics are:

- Always answer within three rings.
- Always call back on any voice messages promptly.
- When someone returns your call, say 'Thank you for returning my call'.

I find the last one very useful. Partly it is a common courtesy, which clients appreciate. But it also gives me two seconds to think 'Who is this?' and to refocus my mind away from another client, or worrying about my tax return or about the grocery shopping. It gives me time to focus 100 per cent on the caller, and to work out who he or she is.

Email and the internet

Here, the client does not even have your tone of voice to react to. Use this to your advantage. It is a chance to create the impression you want to create. Manage your internet presence: assume that your client will check you and your firm out. This means:

- Over-invest in your website: look as large and as professional as you can.
- Review your Facebook and social media presence: if your favourite hobby is getting wildly drunk every weekend and you have the photos to prove it, you will not impress your client.
- Work your Google rankings: do something interesting so that you gain attention and build a presence. The truly desperate have changed their names to something unique, just to come out top on a Google search.
- Be professional in your email and texts: spelling mistakes are not OK. Avoid emoticons, capitalised words and other email classics: these may be fine for students, but they simply make you look unprofessional to most buyers.

● Assume that anything you write will be published to the world and read by the one person you least want to read it. There is no such thing as privacy on the web.

Every interaction with a client creates a good impression or a poor impression. Every text, email and phone call counts. Treat them as seriously as you would treat a face-to-face meeting.

Professional guard

Professional guard is the art of not putting your foot in your mouth and shooting it. It should be obvious: as with much that is obvious, it is routinely missed. Once in a while it pays to refresh the collective discipline of the sales team around professional guard. At sales meetings a 20-minute session on professional guard will help avoid disaster for a few months. The session can be based on the team answering two simple questions:

1   What sort of behaviour do our customers expect of us?

● Turn up to meetings on time.

● Look and dress the part.

● Answer phones within three rings.

● Reply to all messages and emails by close of day at the latest.

● Be positive.

● Don't gossip.

● Don't rubbish the competition.

● Assume that anything you write in an email will be seen and read by the one person you do not want to see it.

● Assume any email you send will be copied to the whole organisation.

● Always deliver on promises.

2 How could we screw up? (This is where war stories of actual and near disaster tend to turn up.)

- Make loose talk about the client.
- Leave confidential papers or data sticks lying around.
- Fail to deliver on promises or follow up on a meeting.
- Forget a client's name.
- Start texting during a client meeting.
- Crash into your client's car in the car park (yes, it has been done and it is not good).
- Get drunk at the corporate hospitality event.
- Win the golf match – by cheating.
- Borrow the CEO's car and get done for speeding in it. (I had an enjoyable day or two explaining that one away.)
- Give two fingers to the Jaguar that nearly runs you down on your bicycle, only to discover that the driver was the CEO and the COO was the passenger. (I was nearly knocked down, but I avoided the two-finger salute. I pretended to laugh with happiness as my life flashed past me.)

Everyone will have their own lists. Most of the items are classic BFO territory: blinding flashes of the obvious. And this is valuable because so often the obvious is ignored. In most cases, the lists will be long and it makes sense to focus on the top ten dos and don'ts, or even just the top five. There is no point in having long lists that no one can remember. Focus on the most important dos and don'ts and stick to them.

Here are two real life examples to illustrate the importance of professional guard:

The train fairy

I was on the train to Newcastle, where I worked for P&G. It was the early morning train and it was likely that a few of the people going from London to Newcastle would be going to P&G, which was a major employer there. Sure enough, I heard a few other people talking about P&G. They were the advertising agency who were going to do a pitch on Fairy Liquid. The problem was that they had not done their work properly and they were still arguing about who was right, who was wrong, who was to blame and how they might get their pitch past P&G. I listened with great interest. I leapt in a taxi to head office, got hold of the Fairy Liquid brand group and debriefed them on what I had heard. By lunchtime I saw an ashen-faced agency emerging from the brand office: they could not believe that the brand manager had been able to read their minds. Careless talk costs contracts.

The Easter bunny

Mobile phones are an invitation to embarrassment. I was minding my own business on the train when a salesperson next to me started talking about a sales fiasco she had had. She was selling Easter eggs to Harrods. Her company could do custom designs for customers, which delighted Harrods. Of course, that meant ordering in sufficient volume. After much haggling, they agreed to an outsize order of 200. The salesperson, who was used to dealing with the likes of Tesco, was moderately pleased. Tesco might order millions, but an order for 200,000 from Harrods was not too bad. Excuse me? Was that 200 or 200,000? The egg maker always quoted with the thousand assumed, so 200 meant 200,000 to the egg maker. To Harrods 200 meant 200. Whoops. At least her indiscrete discussion provided a valuable lesson in the perils of not qualifying customers properly.

Professional guard is more than taking care over what you say where. A session I run with all new account managers, or with new consulting teams, is on professional guard. There are essentially two questions we answer:

- If we were the client, what sort of behaviour would we expect of our supplier?
- How could we really screw up?

The trick here is not to follow some textbook on behaviour: that has all the credibility of an ethics course at Enron. The trick is to get the team members to say what they think is right or wrong: let them own the solution. If it is their solution, they will believe it. If it is the boss's solution, it will be grudgingly observed, but only when the boss is watching.

Conclusion: the sales journey

Success in selling does not come from mastering the most sophisticated sales techniques; success comes from doing the basics exceptionally well. In theory, it is easy to listen, focus on the customer, be positive and do all the other basics of selling. But practice is never as simple as the theory.

To say you need time, experience and practice is not helpful for anyone with wants to progress fast. The random walk of experience can be slow and painful. If we are lucky, we bump into great mentors, but if we are unlucky, we find ourselves being shunted into a career dead end.

There are two ways to get around the problem of time and luck. One way is to learn from your colleagues. They know what works and what does not work in your sales environment. Between you all, you will have encountered nearly every objection, challenge and opportunity that is possible. Tap into that experience and you can dramatically accelerate your learning.

The other way is to use a book like *How to Sell*. It helps take some of the randomness out of the random walk of experience. It puts structure on your experience and helps you understand what works and why it works. It accelerates your journey of discovery. It lets you learn from the accumulated wisdom of thousands of years of experience of other salespeople.

Naturally, we cannot tell what lies ahead of us. To sell is to experience highs and lows, which are higher and lower than what many of our colleagues in cubicle land are likely to experience.

And that is part of the attraction of selling: you live life with the record button on and in full Technicolor. It is a road well worth travelling. But whatever your journey is, enjoy it.

Index

Also by JO OWEN

'A rare gem of a book. Highly recommended.'

John Hempsey, CEO, Moneygram International

'This could easily be the best book on management so far... an entertaining and instructive guide...'

Personnel Today

'Jo Owen, as ever, delivers practical guidance with great good humour and style.'

Professor Nigel Nicholson, London Business School

HOW TO MANAGE, LEAD AND SUCCEED

Jo Owen's practical and straightforward guides show you how to develop the skills and behaviours you need to succeed.